Research: Mohammad Zakwan Nadwi
Art editor: Mateen Ahmad
Graphic design: Mohd. Asjad Ali
Illustrator: Gurmeet

Published in 2016
© Goodword Books 2016

Goodword Books
A-21, Sector 4, Noida-201301, India
Tel. 91120-4314871, +91-8588822674
email: info@goodwordbooks.com
www.goodwordbooks.com

*My First
Prophet
Muhammad ﷺ
Storybook*

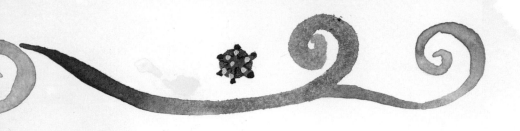

My First
Prophet
Muhammad ﷺ
Storybook

Saniyasnain Khan

Goodword

Contents

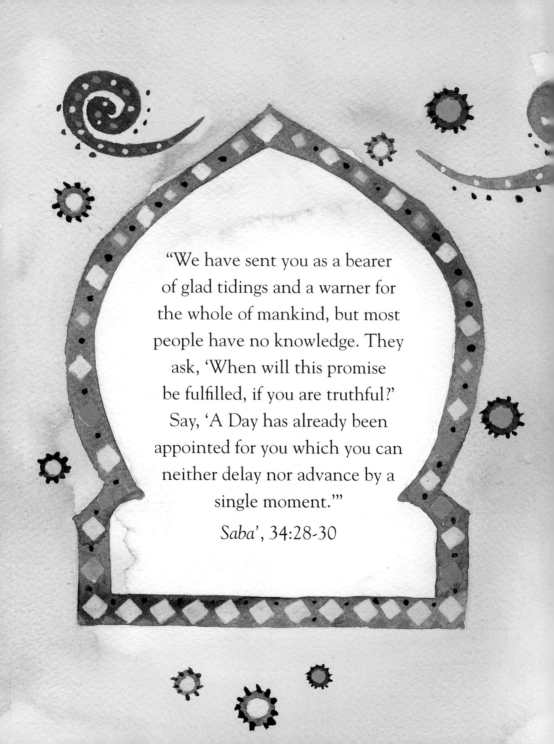

"We have sent you as a bearer of glad tidings and a warner for the whole of mankind, but most people have no knowledge. They ask, 'When will this promise be fulfilled, if you are truthful?' Say, 'A Day has already been appointed for you which you can neither delay nor advance by a single moment.'"

Saba', 34:28-30

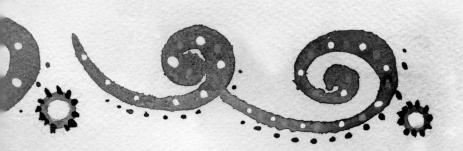

Introduction

In ancient times, when the Prophets Ibrahim ﷺ (Abraham) and Isma'il ﷺ (Ishmael) were building the Kabah in Makkah, they prayed for a prophet among their descendents.

About 2500 years later, the Prophet Muhammad ﷺ, was born from the People of Makkah bringing with him special divine help.

My First Prophet Muhammad ﷺ Storybook takes you back to the early days of Makkah, to a period long before the birth of the Prophet Muhammad ﷺ. It relates fascinating stories about the Kabah and how the pilgrimage to it and trade with far-off lands such as Yemen, Syria, Iraq, Persia were organized along the silk route by the Prophet's great grandfather. Everything is covered from the re-digging of the Zamzam well to the year of elephants, to the birth of the Prophet Muhammad ﷺ, and then on to his childhood in the desert and his early life in Makkah.

Introduction

It tells of how he became a successful
merchant, married Khadija, a wealthy business
woman, and then soon thereafter gave up all
worldly activities in search of the truth. How
he attained prophethood and began his mission
is related in a series of fascinating stories.
Everything is covered from the first revelation of
the Quran by the Archangel Jibril, to the early
preaching of the Prophet and the opposition of
the people of Makkah. This book then goes on
to narrate amazing tales of how Islam began to
spread in Makkah.

My First Prophet Muhammad ﷺ
Storybook shows how, despite
immense opposition and persecution,
the Prophet carried on with his

mission of preaching the message of the one
God. It highlights his patience, dedication,
determination, faith, love, compassion and care
in the face of great odds. It also highlights cases
of some of his early Companions, who, impressed
by Islam's message, accepted the faith. It covers
some of the most significant events in this early
phase of the Prophet's preaching mission,
death of his beloved wife and uncle,
the persecution of Makkan people,
his night journey to Jerusalem and
the seven heavens and finally his migration to
Madinah.

The Prophet Muhammad ﷺ lived his life
as he preached. He remained a patient and
grateful servant of Allah and brought the

message of peace and truth to all mankind.
The life of the Prophet Muhammad ﷺ is an
example for all mankind on how life should
be lived, irrespective of nations or times. He
is an embodiment of all Islamic teachings. He
is a perfect role model. This is expressed in
one of the Prophet's sayings: "Nine things the
Lord has commanded me: Fear of God in
private and in public; Justness, whether
in anger or in calmness; Moderation in
both poverty and affluence; That I should join
hands with those who break away from me; And
give to those who deprive me; And forgive those
who wrong me; And that my silence should
be meditation; And my words remembrance of
God; And my vision keen observation." (*Razin*)

"When Allah created mankind,
He also decreed, 'My mercy
will overcome My anger.'"

Bukhari and Muslim

The History of the Kabah

About 4000 years ago the Prophet Ibrahim (Abraham) ﷺ came to Makkah and settled his family there. His son, Isma'il (Ishmael) ﷺ, grew up and became a great prophet.

The children of the Prophet Isma'il عليه السلام prospered in Makkah and grew in number. Thanks to the Prophet Ibrahim's prayers for Ismail to have many children and the Zamzam spring to appear, many caravans would stop at Makkah on their way to Syria and Yemen.

To help the pilgrims and to look after the various affairs of the Kabah and Makkah, several offices were set up right from the time the Kabah was built.

When Qusayy ibn Kilab took over as the custodian of Kabah, he took on the responsibilities of several of these offices, some of which are as follows: *Hijabah* – Maintenance and keeping the keys of the Kabah; *Siqayah* – Arranging fresh water for the pilgrims; *Rifadah*

– Providing food for the pilgrims; *Nadwah*
– Chairmanship of the meetings held for the
affairs of Makkah; *Qiyadah* – Leadership of the
Makkan army; and *Liwa* – Acting as flag bearer
of Makkah during a campaign or battle.

The Kabah became the central point for
pilgrims from all over Arabia. But the affairs of
the Kabah were not very well organized and the
pilgrims were not taken good care of. Then after
many generations, Qusayy ibn Kilab, became
the Chief of Makkah in the middle of the fifth
century A.D. He was an ancestor of the Prophet
Muhammad ﷺ. Qusayy, being very energetic and
having great leadership qualities, set himself to
organizing the affairs of the Kabah.

Qusayy held many offices of the Kabah such as *hijabah, siqayah, rifadah, nadwah, liwa and qiyadah*.

With his able leadership, the prosperity of Makkah grew by leaps and bounds. His policies gave a boost to trade in Makkah.

Makkah was situated midway on the caravan route to and from Syria and Yemen. For this reason, many caravans would stop at Makkah to rest and trade their goods.

His sincerity and wisdom earned him a very respectable position. Due to his wise policies, the Makkans greatly benefitted and the Quraysh tribe rose to be the most influential tribe of Makkah. Qusayy's position as the Chief of the

Quraysh won him great respect and admiration.

Qusayy would encourage the Quraysh tribe to contribute generously towards the fund for the feeding and care of the pilgrims. He would tell them:

"O people of Quraysh! You live in the neighbourhood of God and His house. The pilgrim is the guest of God and visitor of His house. Of all the guests that you receive during the year, the pilgrim is the most worthy of your hospitality. Provide him with food and drink during the days of pilgrimage."

In this way Qusayy motivated the people of Makkah to come forward and help the pilgrims wholeheartedly.

Before the times of Qusayy ibn Kilab, the houses of Makkah were scattered all around. But, when Qusayy became the chief of Makkah and head of the Quraysh tribe, he ordered that houses to be built near the Kabah. And so the people of Makkah built their houses around the Kabah. Qusayy saw to it that enough space was left for the tawaf – that is, for people to walk all around the Kabah. There were passages and streets leading to the Kabah from all around.

Qusayy also let the Quraysh build their homes nearest to the Kabah and afterwards the houses of other tribes were constructed.

Qusayy had three sons, Abd al-Uzza, Abd Manaf and Abd al-Dar. When Qusayy grew older, he gave his responsibilities to his two sons, Abd Manaf and Abd al-Dar.

Abd al-Dar got the responsibility of the *hijabah* – maintenance of the Kabah and guardianship of the keys of the Kabah. Apart from this, Qusayy also gave him the charge of the *siqayah*, the *liwa'* and the *rifadah*, which meant providing water and food to the pilgrims and bearing the Makkan flag during times of war, etc.

Abd al-Dar took up these responsibilities and discharged them remarkably as his father used to do. For this reason, he was greatly respected and honoured by the people of Makkah.

Abd Manaf had four sons, Hashim, Abd Shams, Al-Muttalib and Nawfal.

After the death of Abd al-Dar, his children took on the responsibilities which their father used to have. But at a point they had some difference with their cousins, the children of Abd Manaf, who also inherited some offices from their father. The dispute was sorted out peacefully and the children of Abd Manaf were given the responsibilities of the *siqayah*, the *rifadah* and the *nadwah*, while the Children of Abd al-Dar were given the responsibilities of the *hijabah* and *liwa'*. And thus peace prevailed in Makkah and a war-like situation was avoided.

Out of the four sons of Abd Manaf, Hashim is very well known. He was the great grandfather of the Prophet Muhammad ﷺ. The Prophet's family is named after him, as they are called the Banu Hashim.

Due to his ability to manage things well, Hashim rose to be the supreme leader of the Quraysh. Like his father, he too urged the Quraysh to be generous to the pilgrims coming to the Kabah, as they were God's guests.

Hashim not only discharged his duties in the best manner as the chief of Makkah, but he also helped the Makkans in a big way.

Once, during a famine in Makkah, Hashim was generous enough not only to feed the pilgrims but also to take care of the entire population of Makkah. This gave him a very high and honourable position.

Apart from this, Hashim organized the trade of Makkah in a big way. He organized two trade caravans, one from Makkah to Syria and another from Makkah to Yemen. These trips were planned very ably by Hashim, one during the summers and the other during the winters.

Under his leadership the Makkans prospered greatly and the economy of the city made great progress.

During the time when Hashim, the great grandfather of the Prophet Muhammad ﷺ, was the Chief of Makkah and the custodian of the Kabah, Makkan trade flourished in a big way.

Hashim planned two great caravans, one

from Makkah to Yemen and the other from Makkah to Syria. One travelled during the summers and the other during the winters. This greatly improved Makkan prosperity. The trade caravans which were travelling from Makkah to Syria and Najd, were connected to the Red Sea from where they were connected to the major trade route of the rest of the world, known as the Silk Route.

The Silk Route or the Silk Road, was a historical network interlinking several trade routes across Asia, Africa, the Mediterranean and Europe.

The Silk Route, which was started by the Chinese more than 2000 years ago, extended from the Red Sea to East Africa, India,

China and Southeast Asia. It was over 6500 kilometers (4000 miles) long and is considered to be a major factor in development of the great civilizations of China, India, Egypt, Iran and Arabia.

Some of the goods traded in those trade caravans were silk, fabrics, musk, perfumes, spices, medicines, jewels, glassware, ivory, textiles, gold, silver, precious stones, etc.

Due to the caravan going from Makkah to Yemen and Syria and from there to other parts of the world, Makkan trade was given a boost and Makkah became the trade centre for the whole of Arabia. Caravans started coming from many countries and goods were exported and imported in big convoys. This gave rise to the

development of markets all around Makkah to deal with the growing business in the region.

Hashim saw to it that business affairs in Makkah developed and the needs of his people in this growing trade were well looked after.

On a trip to Syria, Hashim stopped at Yathrib (now known as Madinah) and there he married a pious lady named Salmah, daughter of 'Amr of the Khazraj tribe. She lived with Hashim at Makkah and later returned to Yathrib where she gave birth to their son named Shaybah.

Some years later, Hashim travelled to Syria on a trade trip. On the way back to Makkah, he fell ill at Ghaza and passed away. He was buried in Ghaza. After the death of Hashim, his brother, Al-Muttalib was appointed as the Chief of the Quraysh tribe and the custodian of the Kabah.

Al-Muttalib was a very kind, noble and generous person. The Quraysh loved him dearly and called him "al-Fayz", or "Mr. Abundance". During his period of being Chief of Makkah, the city continued to flourish and remained peaceful and prosperous.

One day Al-Muttalib thought about his nephew, Shaybah, the son of Hashim. Shaybah lived in Yathrib with his mother. By this time he would be in his youth. Al-Muttalib thought of visiting Yathrib (Madinah) to bring his nephew back to Makkah. So Al-Muttalib travelled all the way to Yathrib and met Salmah, the widow of Hashim and requested her to give his nephew Shaybah, the son of his elder brother Hashim, in his care. Salmah happily handed over Shaybah to Al-Muttalib. So Al-Muttalib set out to return to Makkah along with his nephew, Shaybah, each riding upon a camel.

When both of them riding their respective camels entered Makkah, Shaybah's camel went in front while Al-Muttalib rode behind him. When the people of Makkah saw the two

camels, they recognized Al-Muttalib, but not Shaybah. They thought that this young man must be the slave of Al-Muttalib as he was riding in front of him, so they called out to him, saying, "Ya Abd al-Muttalib," meaning, "O the slave of Al-Muttalib." When Al-Muttalib heard these words, he repeatedly explained to the Makkans that this young man was not his slave, but Shaybah, the son of Hashim.

But due to some confusion, people did not heed Al-Muttalib's explanation and continued to call him Abd al-Muttalib. After some time he was known in Makkah as Abd al-Muttalib, and people completely forgot that his real name was Shaybah. Abd al-Muttalib grew up to be a handsome young man. When his uncle

Al-Muttalib passed away, the Makkans gave Abd al-Muttalib the offices of the *siqayah* and the *rifadah* which his father Hashim had held before his death.

Abd al-Muttalib was a wise man with great insight, resolution and the will to do good works. His main duty was to arrange fresh water for the pilgrims, since the well of Zamzam was no longer functioning. Due to the carelessness of certain people of Jurhum tribe some years ago, the Zamzam well had been filled with sand and mud and was thus so totally ruined that it disappeared. Over the years people did not even know the exact location of the well. However, the Makkans had heard about Zamzam, and the story of the Prophet Ibrahim ﷺ and his son Ismail ﷺ were fresh in their memory. They always desired and hoped that one day the Zamzam well could be restored.

Since Abd al-Muttalib was in charge of arranging fresh water for the pilgrims, he found it difficult to discharge his duties, as there was no well near the Kabah. He had to get water from outside Makkah and store it in a reservoir near the Kabah. For this reason, his desire to restore the Zamzam well grew. One day he had a dream. He saw that someone

in his dream was saying to him to re-dig the
Zamzam well. This gave him confidence in his
idea of re-digging the well of Zamzam, which
was a matter of great concern to him. Abd
al-Muttalib was not aware of the exact location
of the original well, nor could the Makkans
guide him in locating the place where he should
start the digging. With the help of his son
Al-Mughirah, Abd al-Muttalib started the
digging near the Kabah. It was very difficult
work. None of the people of Makkah came

forward to help him. They thought Abd al-
Muttalib's efforts were futile. But he did not
lose his urge to revive the Zamzam well. Then,
after long days of hard work, he was rewarded.
All of a sudden, the water of the Zamzam well

gushed forth from beneath the place where he was digging. This gave immense joy to Abd al-Muttalib as well as to the Makkans.

While digging, Abd al-Muttalib hit upon some rare treasures also. He unearthed two golden gazelles and other precious items. When the Quraysh came to know about this, they wanted the treasures to be handed over to them. But Abd al-Muttalib said, "Let's have a draw."

He suggested three equal partners, namely, the Kabah, the Quraysh, and Abd al-Muttalib. To which the Quraysh agreed.

When the draw of lots were conducted by placing arrows, the Quraysh were completely defeated. The Kabah won the golden gazelles, while Abd al-Muttalib won the other precious

things. Abd al-Muttalib fixed the two golden gazelles at the door of the Kabah as decoration.

Now, since the Zamzam well was restored, the Makkans found it easy to quench their thirst from it and it was easier for Abd al-Muttalib to provide the pilgrims with a supply of fresh water.

Due to the presence of the House of God, the Kabah, a number of people from all over Arabia

would come there to seek the blessings of the idols placed in the Kabah. The pilgrims would make offerings which resulted in great prosperity for the city. Seeing this, there were others who tried to build similar houses of worship in their regions, hoping to divert people from Makkah to their cities. For example, the Gohassanis built a house at Al-Hira. Abraha built a similar house at Yemen. But they failed to attract pilgrims, as no one seemed interested in their houses of worship. The Arabs preferred the ancient house built by the Prophet Ibrahim ﷺ.

Therefore, Abraha, the governor of Yemen, finally decided to destroy the Kabah, built by the Prophet Ibrahim ﷺ, as he felt that this was the only way people from all around Arabia would be diverted to Yemen to the house of worship which he had recently built and decorated beautifully.

So he set out for Makkah with a large army including a number of horses and over a dozen giant elephants.

Certain people tried to stop him from travelling to Makkah with the evil intention of destroying the Kabah. The King of Himyar, Dhu Nafar and the ruler of the Khatham area, Nufail ibn Habib, tried to stop Abraha. But they failed to do so. On the way to Makkah, Abraha stopped at Taif. There one of the leaders of the tribe of Thaqif, whose name was Mas'ud ibn Muattib, assisted him by providing him with a guide whose name was Abu Righal.

Abu Righal escorted Abraha's army and on the way the army encamped at a place called Mughammas, midway between Taif and Makkah. There Abraha sent one of his men, whose name was Aswad ibn Maqsud, to find out more about Makkah and the people living there.

When Aswad ibn Maqsud reached Makkah, people gathered around him. He told the Makkans that Abraha had not come to fight with them. His sole intention in coming there was to destroy the Kabah.

There were many camels, cattle and sheep grazing outside Makkah. Abraha's men took away all the camels and sheep, etc., with them.

They took several camels belonging to Abd al-Muttalib, who was the Chief of Makkah and the grandfather of the Prophet Muhammad ﷺ.

When Abd al-Muttalib came to know about his camels being taken away by Abraha, he went to the place where Abraha had encamped and met him in his tent. Abraha greeted Abd al-Muttalib and met him with honour and respect as Abd al-Muttalib was a great personage.

Abraha said, "What brought you here?"

"You have taken many of my camels," replied Abd al-Muttalib, "I have come to take them back." "But I was expecting that you, being the

Chief of Makkah, would plead with me not to destroy the Kabah," retorted Abraha in wonder. "I have come to destroy the Kabah, and you are talking of your camels," added Abraha in amazement. "I am the lord of the camels, so I have come to take them back," retorted Abd al-Muttalib, "There is a Lord of the Kabah too, and He will save it." Abraha was surprised and became speechless hearing the profound words of Abd al-Muttalib, which were full of wisdom and conviction.

So Abraha allowed him to take his camels. Abd al-Muttalib happily took custody of his camels and left for Makkah.

Upon reaching Makkah, he told the Makkans to leave their homes and go up to the mountains, because Abraha with his enormous army was coming to destroy the Kabah.

The Makkans prayed to Allah to save the Kabah and, as advised by Abd al-Muttalib, they left their hearth and homes and took shelter in the nearby hills.

The next day, Abraha commanded his formidable army to set out towards Makkah at the break of the dawn.

The army slowly marched towards the city of Makkah.

When Abd al-Muttalib saw a huge cloud of dust and sand coming towards him from a distance, he realized that the army of Abraha was now approaching Makkah with the sole intention of destroying the Kabah.

Abd al-Muttalib hastened to the Kabah and took hold of its door handle and prayed vehemently to Allah to save the Kabah from the evil intentions of Abraha, "O Allah, save us from the army. Save us from their evil design. Save our qiblah. If the Kabah is destroyed, we will be destroyed too." With such prayers and deep emotions, Abd al-Muttalib told the Makkans to move out of the city and climb up the mountains as they had no power to fight against the terrifying army of Abraha.

So the people listened to their chief and all of them one by one moved out of their houses—men, women and children—and they climbed the nearby mountains to save themselves from being trampled by the elephants of Abraha.

Abraha's massive army, at the head of which were several large and fierce elephants, approached Makkah. The elephants were roaring with their trunks upward, and the soldiers were chanting and praising their commander and King, Abraha.

Abraha was confident that he would demolish
the Kabah without any resistance from the
people of Makkah. "Who has the
courage to fight against such a massive
army?" thought Abraha.

But all of a sudden, the
elephants who had been
trumpeting in the most
frightening way, stopped moving. The
elephants stood still like statues and refused to
move even one step. The mahouts, who were
driving the elephants, pierced, pricked and
stabbed them with sharp, pointed instruments.
But this had no effect on the elephants. They
stood stock still.

Besides that, flocks of birds flew over the army, carrying pebbles in their beaks and claws.

They showered the pebbles on Abraha's army. Due to this, the whole army was afflicted with a strange disease.

The soldiers were terrified and took flight. The elephants then went berserk and began to trample over them. There was complete disorder and confusion in the army.

Seeing this chaos, Abraha at once decided to order his army to return. So, instead of marching forward and entering Makkah, the army turned and fled towards Yemen. In this miraculous way, Allah saved the Kabah from the evil intentions of Abraha. On the way back to Yemen, many soldiers, horses and elephants began to die.

By the time they reached Sana in Yemen, most of the strong army men had died on the way. Abraha himself fell sick and passed away soon after arriving at his home in Yemen.

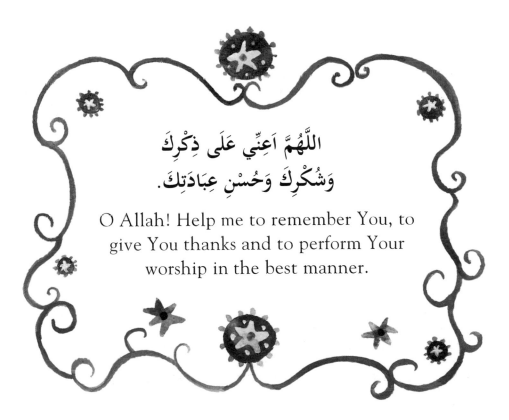

اللَّهُمَّ اَعِنِّي عَلَى ذِكْرِكَ وَشُكْرِكَ وَحُسْنِ عِبَادَتِكَ.

O Allah! Help me to remember You, to give You thanks and to perform Your worship in the best manner.

"Charity does not decrease one's wealth.
Nor does humility lower one's prestige. If
one acts humbly for the sake of God, then
God will certainly raise one's rank."

Muslim

The Birth of the Prophet

Abd al-Muttalib had ten sons, out of which six are well known. They were Al-Abbas, Hamzah, Abu Talib, Abu Lahab, Abdullah and Al-Harith.

Abd al-Muttalib loved Abdullah more than all of his children as he was of an exemplary character, with all the Arab qualities such as honesty, courage, humility and truthfulness.

When Abdullah reached his maturity, Abd al-Muttalib married him to Aminah bint Wahb. She was the daughter Wahb ibn Abd Manaf ibn Zuhrah, the chief of the tribe of Zuhrah.

Abdullah was twenty four years old at the time of his marriage. Soon after the marriage to Aminah, Abdullah went to Syria in a caravan on a trading trip.

On the way back from Syria to Makkah, he fell ill at Madinah and stopped there. When Abd al-Muttalib came to know about the

ill health of his son, he sent his eldest son, Al-Harith to Madinah to bring him back. Abdullah, passed away even before Al-Harith could reach Madinah. Al-Harith returned from Madinah and announced Abdullah's death to the aged Abd al-Muttalib and his bereaved wife Aminah.

A few months later, Aminah gave birth to a baby boy. That was a joyous occasion for Abd al-Muttalib. He carried the new born baby to the Kabah, where he thanked Allah and prayed for the baby's good health.

On the seventh day, Abd al-Muttalib organised an *aqiqah* by inviting relatives to a meal and named the baby "Muhammad".

Since "Muhammad" was an unfamiliar name to the people of Makkah, they asked Abd

al-Muttalib why he had given the baby such an
unusual name. He told them that his grandson
would be praised in the whole world, the
meaning of the word, "Muhammad" being "the
praised one".

The Prophet Muhammad ﷺ was born on
20th April, 570 A.D., in the city of Makkah.
The Prophet Muhammad's birth took place
in the same year in which Abraha planned
an attack on Makkah with his evil intention
of destroying the Kabah. This month became
known as the Year of the Elephant.

The Prophet Muhammad ﷺ once said that
Allah chose Isma'il ﷺ from among the Children
of Ibrahim ﷺ. Then Allah chose Kananah from
among the Children of Isma'il ﷺ. Then Allah

chose the Quraysh from among the Children of Kananah. Then Allah chose the Banu Hashim from among the Quraysh. Then, finally, Allah chose Muhammad ﷺ from among the Banu Hashim.

According to Sahih al-Bukhari, the following is the lineage of the Prophet Muhammad ﷺ. Muhammad ibn Abdullah ibn Abd al-Muttalib ibn Hashim ibn Abd Munaf ibn Qusayy ibn Kilab ibn Murrah ibn Kab ibn Luwi ibn Ghalib ibn Fihr ibn Malik ibn Nasr ibn Nianah ibn Huzimah ibn Mudrikah ibn Ilyas ibn Mudar ibn Nizar ibn Maz ibn Adnan.

In those days, it was the custom for the townspeople to send their new born babies to a Bedouin nurse to be brought up in desert. Many families living in the desert as nomads, known as Bedouin or desert Arabs, were providing this service.

After the birth of the Prophet Muhammad ﷺ, his mother, Aminah too decided to send the baby to the Banu S'ad tribe. First Aminah gave the baby to Thuwaybah, who nursed him till the wet nurses of Banu S'ad arrived in Makkah. Thuwaybah was the maid of the Prophet's uncle, Abu Lahab. She also nursed the Prophet's uncle Hamzah. Though Thuwaybah nursed the Prophet just for a few days, the Prophet held her in great esteem and respect till she passed away.

After some days, the wet nurses of the Banu S'ad tribes arrived at Makkah to take charge of infants and take them to their desert home for nursing and suckling.

Halima Sadia tells of how along with several other women she arrived at Makkah in search of a child to take him for nursing. No one was interested in taking charge of the little Muhammad, as he was an orphan. When the ladies came to know that his father was dead, they refused him, as they expected a reward from the father when they returned the child after nursing him. Halima Sadia says that by the evening all the women had got children for suckling except herself. So when the time came to return to their homes, she said to

her husband, Harith ibn Abdul Uzza, "I am
not feeling good about returning home with
my friends without taking along a child. So I
want to go back and take that orphan child."
Her husband said, "I think there is no harm in
doing so. Maybe Allah will bless us for this."
Therefore, Halima Sadia went to the house of
the baby Muhammad. His mother, Aminah then
entrusted him to Halima Sadia and she took him
with her to be nursed in the desert.

The Prophet Muhammad ﷺ at that very
young age spent little more than two years
with the family of Halima Sadia in the desert.
The little Muhammad would play freely

with Halima's daughter, Shayma, in the vast expanse of the desert under the beautiful sky and surrounded by the beauties of nature. The pure air of the desert and natural environment helped the Prophet to grow up to be a strong and healthy child.

After the completion of two years and a few months, Halimah Sadia brought back the little Muhammad to his mother at Makkah.

These years were full of blessings and happiness for the family of Halima Sadia.

Her herds of sheep and goats miraculously grew in number. And everything in her household seemed to prosper and flourish. Her heart was brimming over with happiness. Halima knew that this was all due to the blessed child, Muhammad ﷺ.

When Muhammad ﷺ was six, Aminah decided to take him with her to visit his uncles in Yathrib. Yathrib (now known as Madinah) was situated in the midst of volcanic hills in the Hijaz region of western Saudi Arabia about 160 kilometers (100 miles) inland from the Red Sea. In its early days, it was an oasis famed for the dates from its palm groves.

It was a long journey by caravan, but young Muhammad ﷺ enjoyed meeting his cousins, playing with them and learning to swim. Muhammad ﷺ and Aminah enjoyed the pleasant climate and the company of their relatives for a month. But, tragically, on the journey back to Makkah, Aminah fell ill and died. Little Muhammad ﷺ returned home with Aminah's maid, Barakah.

Muhammad's grandfather adopted him and took care of him. Abd al-Muttalib loved Muhammad ﷺ dearly, and was convinced that he was destined for greatness. Muhammad ﷺ sat by Abd al-Muttalib's side near the Kabah during all his consultations, and when Abd

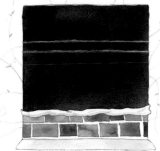

al-Muttalib fell sick two years later, Muhammad ﷺ tended him faithfully. When his grandfather died, Muhammad was adopted by his uncle, Abu Talib. Muhammad ﷺ became part of Abu Talib's large family right away, and was his uncle's favourite.

When Aminah, the mother of the Prophet Muhammad ﷺ passed away, he was just six years old. His father passed away even before he was born. Now with the death of his mother, the Prophet became completely orphaned.

After the death of the Prophet's mother, his grandfather, Abd al-Muttalib took him under his care and guardianship. Abd al-Muttalib greatly loved him and was sure that this young boy had a great future. It was he who named him "Muhammad", meaning "the Praised One."

Abd al-Muttalib was the Chief of the Quraysh tribe. He was the custodian of the Kabah. He would sit on a special cushion laid out for him near the Kabah. Sometimes the Prophet Muhammad ﷺ would come to see him there, and would sit on the cushion. People would tell him not to sit there, but Abd al-Muttalib would stop them saying, "Let him sit. My child's future is very bright."

Whenever Abd al-Muttalib asked him to go and do some work, he would do it with great care and responsibility. One day, one of Abd al-Muttalib's camels was lost. He asked the Prophet Muhammad ﷺ, who was about eight years old, to go and search for the camel. The Prophet went to search for it, but did not return for a long time. Abd al-Muttalib became very restless. He started doing rounds (*tawaf*) of the Kabah and started praying for the safety of his grandson.

Soon after, the Prophet returned with the camel. Abd al-Muttalib said, sighing with relief,

"My child, I got restless, as a mother gets restless when her child gets lost."

Soon afterwards, when the Prophet Muhammad ﷺ was about eight years old, Abd al-Muttalib fell ill and passed away. Abd al-Muttalib was eighty-five years old at the time of his death.

Before his death, Abd al-Muttalib called his son, Abu Talib, and told him to take the Prophet Muhammad ﷺ into his care and protection. The Prophet was eight years old at that time. From the age of eight till the age of twenty-five, the Prophet lived at the house of Abu Talib.

Though Abu Talib was not rich, he was a very kind-hearted person. He took great care in the upbringing of the Prophet and remained his greatest helper and supporter throughout his life.

When the Prophet Muhammad ﷺ was twelve years old, Abu Talib was preparing a trade caravan to Syria. He was about to carry his goods to be sold in Syrian markets.

When the Prophet learnt about his uncle's Syrian visit, he too showed interest in visiting Syria along with him. Though the Prophet was barely twelve years old at that time, seeing his interest and enthusiasm, Abu Talib agreed to take him in the caravan to Syria. The caravan stopped at the city of

Busra in Syria. There a Christian scholar by the name of Buhaira saw the Prophet Muhammad ﷺ. He immediately recognized him by some signs, which he had read in the religious books about the Last Prophet who was about to born in Arabia. He invited Abu Talib and the Prophet to a dinner.

After the meal, he asked Abu Talib, "Who is this boy?" Abu Talib said, "He is my son." Buhaira said, "No, he cannot be your son." His father must have passed away long ago. Abu Talib said, "You are right, he is my nephew. His name is Muhammad. His father passed away even before he was born. Then Buhaira explained that he had noticed some signs in this child and said, "He will become the last

Prophet." He further told Abu Talib to return to Makkah quickly, because if people saw him they might recognize him and try to harm him.

Hearing the words of Buhaira, Abu Talib quickly sold his goods in the Syrian markets and lost no time in returning to Makkah. His main concern was the safety of his nephew, Muhammad.

In the early years of his youth, the Prophet Muhammad ﷺ would take the herds of sheep and goats of the people of Makkah outside the city to let them graze. In this way, the Prophet started earning at a young age. His uncle Abu Talib, under whose care the Prophet was living, was not very rich, so the Prophet worked as a shepherd to earn a living.

In later days the Prophet told his Companions that there was no Prophet who had ever lived on this earth, who had not worked as a shepherd. The Companions asked in surprise, "You too, O Prophet" To which the Prophet said, "Yes, I too."

When a person goes in to the forest and the fields with herds of cattle and sheep, it is like coming close to nature.

There he thinks about creation, the natural beauty of vast mountains. And the open sky inspires him to come closer to the Creator. So he starts having divine inspirations which help in his spiritual growth and uplift.

When the Prophet Muhammad ﷺ took the sheep and goats outside Makkah to let them graze for hours and hours, he would remain immersed in thoughts of the creation and the purpose of life. He would think about the Creator, the existence of man and the life beyond. Slowly, he begins to understand the meaning of life. His mind and soul begin to find answers to the questions which have always surged in his mind.

Allah was then preparing him for a bigger

role—the role of the Prophethood to humanity.

When the Prophet Muhammad ﷺ was about fifteen years old, a war broke out in Makkah between the tribes of the Banu Qays and the Quraysh. This war was known as harb al-fujar. The war went on for several years. Due to the destruction and aftermath of the war, the atmosphere of peace and prosperity was shattered in Makkah.

Makkah had been an abode of peace for centuries. People from all around Arabia used to visit the holy city on pilgrimages and for trade. But the war shattered the peace and tranquillity of the city. Trade and business were particularly hit. People would not deal with honesty as they used to do. This gave a bad name to the holy city of Makkah.

A man came from Yemen to sell his goods in Makkah. He sold his goods to Al-'Aas ibn Wa'il, but was not given the agreed amount for them. So he wrote a poem in which he said that he had been cheated by a Makkan trader. He mocked the Makkans about how bad their character had become. Hearing his chiding words, many Makkans thought something must be done, as their reputation was at stake.

Taking into account these sentiments, Zubayr ibn Abdul Muttalib called a meeting at the house of Abdullah ibn Judan. Many people gathered and aired their views about how to improve the tarnished image of the Makkah.

They pledged to revive the old pact, which was known as the Alliance of Fudul. This pact had long ago been established by Fadl ibn Fudala, Fadl ibn Wada'a and Fudayl ibn Harith to help the oppressed people. But after their death this pact had become non-functional.

Now they pledged to revive this alliance to help the oppressed people by putting pressure on the oppressors and the guilty who did not give their dues to people, especially those who came from other places to Makkah. The Prophet Muhammad ﷺ was also present in the meeting which took place at the house of Abdullah ibn Judan. The Prophet was about twenty years old at that time. Later, in the years of his prophethood, the Prophet said, "Even today, if I am called to the Alliance of Fudul, I will surely go and help the oppressed people."

When the Prophet Muhammad ﷺ grew up and attained his youth, he became known as an honest and hardworking man. Due to these qualities, Khadijah, daughter of Khuwaylid hired him to go to Syria to sell her goods in the Syrian trade markets.

The Prophet Muhammad ﷺ was happy with the opportunity and looked forward to the new venture. He was twenty-five years old and full of enthusiasm. He wanted to make something of himself and was proud to be in charge of a caravan of many camels loaded with precious goods. He was confident that he would manage the long journey and sell the goods in Syria at a good profit. He wanted to prove himself and show that he could do his job well.

He had made this journey once earlier with his uncle Abu Talib. That time he was just twelve years old but he still remembered the trip well. Then, too, they were carrying goods to be sold in the Syrian markets. This time, however, things were a bit different. He was older and he was in charge. Everything depended on his planning.

To succeed he had to work hard and take good care of the camels and the goods given to him. There was no scope for a mistake, because the goods were not his own but entrusted to him by a trusting woman.

To help him with his work, Khadijah sent her loyal servant, Maysarah, to go with him.

The journey from Makkah to Syria was very long and demanding. One had to have a lot of stamina and a strong will to undertake it. At first they travelled for many days through the scorching sands. They crossed one ridge of dunes after another and still it looked as if the desert would never end. But, finally, they left

the desert behind and reached lands which were more welcoming. Now they were crossing shady green forests and meadows with cool streams. The animals could drink sweet water and graze on fresh grass. In the end they arrived in Syria.

The market town was even bigger than what the Prophet remembered from his childhood. There were hundreds of animals, camels, horses, oxen and mules everywhere—all of them bringing goods from faraway lands. Hundreds of merchants were busy displaying their wares and even more people were milling around to look at the goods on display.

With the help of Maysarah, the Prophet found a nice spot for his camels, not far away from a clump of shady trees and a short distance away from the watering place. They tethered the camels and unloaded the goods they had brought. Soon they were surrounded by merchants curious to see what they had. In no time they sold all the merchandise for a good profit, with the Prophet holding on to each piece till he got the best price for it.

Once they had disposed of the things they had brought with them, they decided to shop for goods to take back home. Before deciding what to buy, the Prophet left Maysarah in charge of the camels and went around the market to see what was there.

He visited each stall more than once, comparing the prices and quality. He talked to many merchants with great politeness but bargained hard if he liked something he thought

would sell well in the markets of Makkah. In those days, the markets of Syria were full of goods coming from all over the known world.

There were traders from Turkey, China, India, Uzbekistan and Tajikistan displaying their wares in the shops. Besides articles of everyday use, one could buy ivory, gold, silver, precious stones and jewellery, beautiful fabrics made of cotton and silk, spices and perfumes and even delicate items made of glass.

After looking at all the things in the market, the Prophet bought those that would sell best in Makkah: jewellery for women, toys and trinkets for children, beautiful fabrics for all and things for the house: pots and pans, tasty foodstuffs and sweets, and medicines for the sick and elderly.

When the caravan reached Makkah, everybody noticed that the camels were carrying huge loads. People were really curious to see what the Prophet had got from Syria. However, the caravan did not stop at the market place but went straight to Khadijah's house.

The Prophet gave Khadijah all the goods he had brought from Syria and all the money he had made by selling her goods there.

Khadijah was amazed at the quantity of goods and the amount of money in cash. Never before had any trade caravan brought her that much profit. It was more than double what she used to earn earlier. And it was all due to the truthfulness and honesty of the Prophet!

On top of that, Maysarah, her servant, who had accompanied the caravan to Syria, praised the Prophet in glowing terms to anybody who would listen and he also told Khadija again and again: "I have never met anybody more honest or more trustworthy than Abu Talib's nephew."

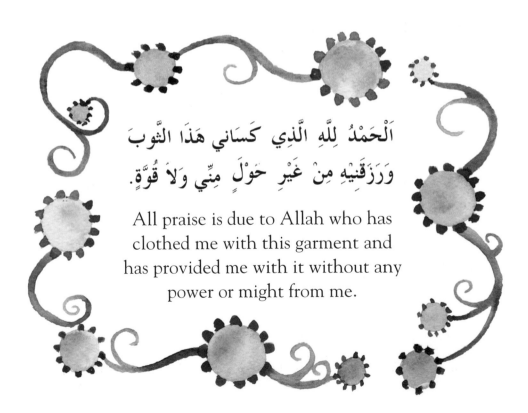

اَلْحَمْدُ لِلَّهِ الَّذِي كَسَانِي هَذَا الثَّوبَ
وَرَزَقَنِيهِ مِنْ غَيْرِ حَوْلٍ مِنِّي وَلاَ قُوَّةٍ.

All praise is due to Allah who has clothed me with this garment and has provided me with it without any power or might from me.

"Among the believers who show
the most perfect faith are those
who have the best disposition
and are kindest to their families."

Tirmidhi

The Prophet Marries Khadija

The Prophet Muhammad ﷺ had been used to working for his living since his early youth. By the time he was 25 years old, he was already well known as an honest and hard-working person. Impressed by these qualities,

Khadija bint Khuwaylid, a wealthy widow of Makkah, hired him to lead her caravan to Syria and sell her goods in the Syrian markets.

The Prophet Muhammad ﷺ had already made a journey to Syria once earlier with his uncle and he knew the route. He organized the caravan carrying the goods entrusted to him by Khadija very well and once in Syria, conducted the business with great foresight and wisdom, making a fortune for Khadija.

When the Prophet Muhammad ﷺ returned to Makkah, Khadija was very pleased with the way he had conducted his business in Syria and could not believe that he had made so much money for her. She was extremely impressed by his truthful ways and his honest dealings. His persona and pleasing personality made a favorable impression on her and she said to herself:

"I have never met anybody more honest and more trustworthy than Abu Talib's nephew."

Khadija began to pay close attention to the Prophet and realized that all the people in Makkah liked him a lot and he had many friends. He was hard-working, honest and trustworthy. She liked that. She also liked his simple and unaffected ways. She thought to herself: "He is the best man I have ever met in my life."

One day one of her best friends, Nafisa bint Munya, came to meet her. They sat together and talked. Then the conversation turned to Khadija's last business venture, the Syrian caravan and the goods it had brought. Khadija remarked: "I have never made so much money in any of my earlier ventures. I think I was very lucky to have hired Abu Talib's nephew. He managed to sell my goods in Syria for a very good price and whatever he bought with that money and brought to Makkah fetched me a handsome profit as well. He has good business sense and on top of that he is a good and sensible man."

Her friend agreed with her and said: "Yes, you were very lucky indeed."

And then a sudden thought struck her: "He is a young man of marriageable age and you are a widow. You are well suited to each other. Why don't you marry him? I can act as the go-between."

Khadija thought for a while and agreed with her: "You are right. It is a good idea. Help me with this and go and talk to him."

Nafisa went straight to the Prophet Muhammad ﷺ and asked him: "Why don't you get married?"

He answered truthfully: "I don't have money to get married. I cannot support a family as yet."

But Nafisa would not give up. She asked: "What if you are let off from taking on such a responsibility?"

"How could that be possible?" asked the Prophet, wondering what she could mean.

"That is simple and easy. Khadija would like to marry you," explained Nafisa.

This was a pleasant surprise for the Prophet. He had great regard for Khadija and held her in high esteem. He liked the idea of marrying her and promised Nafisa: "I will talk to my uncle and let you know what he thinks."

Abu Talib, the Prophet's uncle, was very pleased when he heard of the marriage proposal. With great joy he immediately agreed to it. The Prophet was happy, too, and in no time the day for the marriage ceremony was fixed. The marriage became a good occasion for the family and friends to get together. In the presence of the family, Abu Talib read the nikah himself. Khadija's father was dead, so her uncle, Amr ibn Asad, was there instead as was her learned cousin, Waraqah ibn Nawfal. The Prophet's foster mother, Halima Sadia, was there too.

For a few days after the nikah the Prophet and Khadija lived at the house of Abu Talib. Then Khadija bought a house from her nephew, Hakim ibn Hizam, and they moved there.

The new house into which the Prophet Muhammad ﷺ and Khadija moved was very nice, though not very big.

But it had enough space for everybody. It even had a little walled courtyard behind the house where they could sit after sunset.

The Prophet Muhammad ﷺ and Khadija did not live by themselves in their new house. There were many more people who lived with them. First of all, there was Umm Ayman, the old maid of Amina, the Prophet's mother, who had brought him up after his mother died. The Prophet was very fond of her because she reminded him of his childhood and his mother.

Then there was Zayd ibn Haritha, a slave whom Khadija gave to her husband to help him with his work. But the Prophet, who was very kind and disliked any sort of oppression, immediately freed Zayd ibn Haritha and treated

him like his own son. Zayd ibn Haritha loved the Prophet so much that when his own family came to take him back home, he refused to go with them because he did not want to be parted from the Prophet. He stayed on with the Prophet for many years to come.

Later on, when his own father died, Zubayr ibn Awwam also came to stay with the Prophet and Khadija and became one of the first people to accept Islam.

The Prophet and Khadija had six children, two boys and four girls. Unfortunately, both the boys, Qasim and Abdullah, died when they were still little babies.

The four daughters: Zaynab, Ruqayya, Umm Kulthum and Fatima, grew up into beautiful young girls and were married when the time came.

Zaynab was married to Khadija's nephew, Abu al-As ibn Rabia, the son of Khadija's sister. He was a kind and upright man and they were very happy together.

Ruqayya and Umm Kulthum were married to two sons of Abu Lahab, Utbah and Utaybah. But when the Prophet Muhammad ﷺ began his mission of spreading the message of Islam, Abu Lahab, though also an uncle of the Prophet, became the Prophet's enemy. Also, most of the members of the Quraysh, the main tribe of Makkah, opposed the Prophet. In these circumstances the Quraysh and Abu Lahab forced Utbah and Utaybah to divorce the daughters of the Prophet and send them back to their father. Later on Ruqayya was married to Uthman ibn Affan. When things in Makkah became difficult for the believers, both of them, together with some other followers of Islam, migrated to Abyssinia, now known as Ethiopia, in Africa, and stayed there for about two years. When the Prophet left Makkah and settled in Madina, they came back and joined him there. Some time before the battle of Badr, Ruqayya fell sick and died soon after. After her death, the Prophet married his other daughter, Umm Kulthum, to Uthman ibn Affan, but she too did not live long.

The youngest daughter, Fatima, married her father's cousin and son of Abu Talib, Ali. They had two sons, Hasan and Husain. The Prophet loved his grandsons very much and playing with them gave the Prophet a lot of joy.

Marriage with Khadijah gave the Prophet an opportunity to lead a comfortable life as a wealthy and respected noble of Makkah. And, indeed, for a few years the Prophet Muhammad ﷺ led an uneventful and quiet life of a merchant ﷺ. However, though busy with his business activities, the Prophet always found time to think about things other than what everyday life brought in its daily routine. Finally, a time came when he gave up all worldly activities and set out to search for the truth.

Since his early years the Prophet liked to spend time alone and try to answer the questions coming to his mind: "Who has made this world? Why are people born and why do they die? What is the meaning of their lives? And how to reach the ultimate Truth?"

The Prophet knew that these questions had answers.

But the answers could not be found in the bustle of daily life. So he began to take time off from his everyday pursuits. Instead of meeting people all the time in their homes and at gatherings, and trying to gain for himself a position among the nobles of Makkah, the Prophet Muhammad ﷺ would wander into the barren hills of the desert. He would sit for hours in the wilderness and ponder upon the mysteries of creation. The vast silence of the desert, with its seemingly endless sand and clear sky and at night, equally endless darkness, alive only with the twinkling of millions and millions of tiny stars, seemed to bring one very close to the Creator.

Often the Prophet Muhammad ﷺ would climb up the mountain called Jabal al-Nur, or the Mountain of Light, three miles away from Makkah. Near the top of this mountain there was a cave called the Cave of Hira. This was his favorite retreat and he loved to sit there and contemplate the view in front of him. When the night came, the Prophet would look at the sky sparkling with stars and would be filled with wonder at its grandeur. He could spend many days in this manner, coming back home only to get more food and water. There was nothing he loved more than the solitude of nature to pray and meditate in, asking the Maker of the heavens and earth for the answers to all the questions that surged in his mind: "What is man's true role in life? What does the Lord require of us, His servants?"

In the year 610 A.D., the Prophet Muhammad ﷺ, now forty years of age, went as was his habit to the Cave of Hira to spend Ramadan, the traditional month of retreat. He was sitting all alone in this cave, when he had an extraordinary experience.

One day, after many days of the Prophet's meditation, the Archangel Jibril, or Gabriel, suddenly appeared before the Prophet Muhammad ﷺ in human form.

"Read!" commanded the angel.

"I cannot read," the Prophet Muhammad ﷺ protested.

So the angel held the Prophet Muhammad ﷺ tightly by the shoulders, shook him, and taught him these words:

"Read: In the name of your Lord who created, created man from a clot. Read: And your Lord is the Most Generous who taught by the pen, taught man what he did not know." (Al-'Alaq, 96:1-5.)

These were the first words of the Revelation. The Prophet Muhammad ﷺ felt that these lines were actually being written in his heart.

But the experience left him surprised and confused. He even felt he might be falling ill. Gradually, the Prophet Muhammad began to understand—his quest for truth has finally been rewarded. His restless, searching soul has been joined with his Lord.

Allah not only gave him guidance, but He also chose the Prophet Muhammad ﷺ as His Prophet and special Messenger, to bring His word to a world that had gone badly astray. It was a tremendous responsibility. But the Prophet Muhammad ﷺ, far from becoming vain or proud, remained as good and humble a man as ever.

The Prophet Muhammad ﷺ continued to receive divine revelations from time to time over the next twenty-three years. The Archangel Jibril would come to him in different forms, sometimes huge and filling the horizon, and sometimes just a pair of eyes watching him. Sometimes he remained invisible. Occasionally only his voice could be heard. Sometimes the voice was muffled, like a ringing in the Prophet Muhammad's head. But the meaning was always clear.

The Prophet Muhammad ﷺ could neither make the revelations happen, nor could he stop them. They could descend on him at any time. They used to happen while he was making a speech, while sitting, while praying, or even while riding his camel. He always knew when they were about to take place and his Companions could see the change come over him. He would become silent and normally would lie down wrapped up in his cloak. His face might become red and he would perspire profusely, even on cold days. His Companions said that if one were near him, one could hear something like humming around his face.

The experience of the revelations always seemed to make the Prophet Muhammad ﷺ feel close to death, as if he was leaving his body and might never return. "Not once did I receive a revelation without thinking that my soul had been torn away," said the Prophet.

At the end of the experience, the Prophet Muhammad ﷺ would return to normal and recite the newly revealed verses of the Quran.

His Companions were instructed to memorize them and record them.

The experience in the Cave of Hira shook the Prophet to his core. He did not know what to make of it. Disturbed and frightened, he went straight home and told Khadija about the incident. He said:

"Khadija, I do not understand what has happened to me. I fear for my life."

Seeing him trembling in shock and distress, Khadija put a blanket over him and comforted him, saying:

"Allah will never let you down. You are kind to your family. You are truthful. You help the needy and the poor. You gladly welcome anybody who comes as a guest to your house.

You follow the way of truth and justice. There is nothing for you to fear."

When the Prophet finally fell asleep, Khadija hurried straight to Waraqah ibn Nawfal, her cousin, for advice. Waraqah was a very learned and spiritual man and Khadija trusted his judgment. She told him about what had happened in the cave of Hira and wanted to know what he thought of it all. Having heard her account, Waraqah said:

"If what you say is true, there is no doubt, this must have been the very same angel that visited the Prophets Musa عليه السلام and Isa عليه السلام."

Later on, Khadija took the Prophet to meet Waraqah. The Prophet told him of his experience in the cave. After listening to his words, Waraqah said:

"You will be the Prophet to this nation."

He promised that if he were still alive, he would help in the mission of the Prophet. But Waraqah, being an old, blind man, passed away soon after.

Gradually, the Prophet began to understand the meaning of the revelation. At the same time, he realized that a great responsibility of

spreading the message of the Quran to all people had fallen on his shoulders.

It was the year 610 AD. The Prophet Muhammad ﷺ was then 40 years old and he and Khadija had been married for 15 years.

At first the mission of spreading Islam was confined to his close relatives. Only later on did Allah command the Prophet to take the message to people at large.

Khadija was the first person to accept Islam. She took no time acknowledging the Prophet and believing in him. She had always known him to be trustworthy and truthful.

One day, the angel Jibril came to the Prophet and taught

him how to perform the ablution (*wudu*). He then taught the Prophet how to say the prayer (*salah*). To make sure that he remembered all the movements and words properly, the Prophet said his prayers for the first time alongside the angel Jibril. Later on the Prophet went home and taught wudu and salah to Khadija. Thereafter, accompanied by Khadija, the Prophet started to pray in his own house.

One day, his cousin, Ali ibn Abi Talib, who was just ten years old, visited their house as usual and saw the Prophet and Khadija praying together. He was surprised and asked:

"What is this? I have never seen anybody doing this before."

The Prophet explained to his little cousin:

"We are saying prayers, or salah. Allah has made me His Prophet and revealed the Quran to me. Why don't you join us?"

Ali took in the words and decided to think over the whole matter. The next day he came again to their house and said:

"I want to join you. I accept Islam and want to follow its teachings."

Thus Ali became the second believer after Khadija.

From that time on, the Prophet would lead the prayers and Ali would stand next to him with Khadija standing behind them. They were the only three people offering *salah*.

At that time only two prayers, Fajr and Isha, each with two *rak'ahs*, were prescribed.

After receiving the first revelation of the Quran, the Prophet received the second revelation. It was the beginning of chapter 74, al-Muddaththir. It commanded the Prophet to call people to God and tell them of the creation plan of the Creator.

The Prophet knew what was expected of him and immediately planned to work for dawah. His wife, Khadija, and his cousin, Ali ibn Abi Talib, had already accepted Islam. Then there was Zayd ibn Haritha, a former slave whom Khadija had gifted to the Prophet. Zayd ibn Haritha also lived with the Prophet and assisted him in his work. The Prophet treated him as his own son. When the Prophet invited Zayd to accept Islam, Zayd lost no time in entering the fold of Islam. Afterwards the Prophet explained the message of Islam to his four daughters, Zaynab, Umm Kulthum, Ruqayyah and Fatima. They too immediately accepted Islam. In this way, the Prophet's entire family came into the fold of Islam.

All these people would read whatever portion of the Quran was revealed, and would pray to Allah as taught by the Prophet. Also, they would together plan to do dawah among the citizens of Makkah.

One day, Abu Bakr ibn Abi Quhafa left his house and went to meet his childhood friend, the Prophet Muhammad ﷺ. When Abu Bakr came to the Prophet, he said, "O Abul Qasim, these days don't see you in the meetings of the Makkan people. People blame you for having abandoned our deities. Also I heard that you believe our forefathers and elders were fools and misguided."

The Prophet answered, "Yes, it is true. I am the Prophet of God, and I invite you to believe in one God and I call you to be obedient to Him."

He further added, "By God, this is the truth. You should not associate anyone as an equal to

Allah and should worship Him alone."

After that the Prophet recited some verses of the Quran.

Abu Bakr was overwhelmed with emotion. He immediately testified to the authenticity of the Prophet Muhammad's prophethood and accepted Islam.

The Prophet became so happy when Abu Bakr embraced Islam, that there was no one as happy as he was in the whole of Makkah. Even after many years, the Prophet would often say, "Everyone whom I had invited to Islam was filled with some kind of hesitation but Abu Bakr accepted my message at once and without any doubt."

It was for this quality that Abu Bakr was known as Siddiq, "the one who testifies to the truth".

After accepting Islam, Abu Bakr asked the Prophet, "Now, tell me, what is my work to be?"

The Prophet replied, "The same work for which I have been sent forth." Meaning, calling people to God or doing dawah work. Abu Bakr was a very gentle, kind and noble man, therefore he was well liked by the people. He had a good knowledge of history and genealogy – knowledge of the families and their forefathers – and was greatly admired for his good memory and wisdom. Also, because he was a tradesman, many people knew him well.

Abu Bakr was already 36 years old at that time, so he planned to do dawah work in an organized manner. He started dawah work among the people he knew and, due to his efforts, a number of people accepted Islam. Some of the notable names and the age of each person at that time is given below:

Uthman ibn Affan – 34 years old,

Abdul Rahman ibn Awf – 30 years old,

Sa'd ibn Abi Waqqas – 27 years old,

Zubayr ibn al-Awwam – 22 years old,

Talha ibn Ubaydullah – 13 years old.

Abu Bakr brought these people to meet the Prophet. They all accepted Islam and joined the mission of the Prophet, giving it much strength in the early period.

Under the guidance of the Prophet and Abu Bakr, these people began to spread the teachings of Islam in Makkah. As a result of their efforts, many more people entered the fold of Islam. Some of the names are as follows: Abu Ubaydah ibn al-Jarrah; Ubaydah ibn Harith ibn Abdul Muttalib; Uthman ibn Maz'un; Arqam ibn Abi al-Arqam; Fatimah bint al-Khattab (sister of Umar ibn Khattab); Sa'id ibn Zayd; Asma bint Abu Bakr and Khabbah ibn Arat.

After some time, yet another group of people entered the fold of Islam due to the dawah work of those who had already accepted Islam.

Some of the names of this group are as follows: Umayr ibn Abi Waqqas; Abdullah ibn Mas'ud; Abdullah ibn Jahsh; Ja'far ibn Abi Talib and his wife Asma; Khalid ibn Sa'id ibn al-'As; 'Ammar ibn Yasir and Bilal ibn Rabah al-Habashi.

With this the total number of Muslims in Makkah rose to 40. This included men, women and children. Now, Islam had come into the limelight in Makkah and people were beginning to talk about it a lot.

اللَّهُمَّ إِنِّي أَسْأَلُكَ عِلْماً نَافِعاً وَرِزْقاً
وَاسِعاً وَشِفَاءً مِنْ كُلِّ دَاءٍ.

O Allah I ask of You beneficial
knowledge, abundant provision, and
a cure from all disease.

"One who does not show mercy
to our juniors and respect to our
elders is not one of us."

Tirmidhi

The Beginning of Difficult Times

Arqam ibn al-Arqam, a sixteen-year-old youth, who had recently accepted Islam, lived near the Safa hillock. His house was a bit isolated and there were no neighbours looking to see who came there. It was therefore easy for the Companions to come there whenever they wanted.

This house became the first centre in which to carry out dawah activities. Here the people would meet and recite whatever portions of the Quran were revealed till that times. The Prophet would personally instruct people to write and commit the Quran to memory. He would also explain to them the verses so that they might understand their meaning. In this way, the house of Arqam, which was known as Dar al-Arqam, became the first training centre of Islam.

As Dar al-Arqam was at a distance from the other houses in Makkah, for a long time

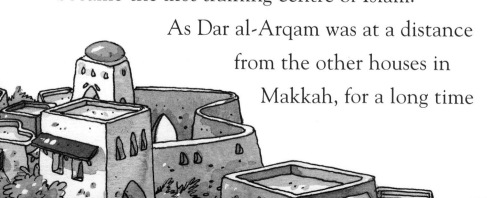

the Quraysh had no idea that the Prophet and his Companions gathered there and conducted their meetings.

The only curriculum for the training of the companions in Dar al-Arqam was the Quran, which was incomplete at that point of time, as it was still in the process of being revealed. The Quran was the only literature of the Prophet's mission. It contained the fundamental profession of faith and was the handbook of prayer and worship. It mentioned Paradise, Hell and accountability on the Day of Judgment. In this way, the Quran became the first and only textbook for the training of the Companions and preparing the first team of da'is (those who call people to God) to take forward the message of Islam. This first team of Companions was able to successfully spread the message of Islam in Makkah.

Due to their efforts, in almost all the tribes in Makkah there were people who came into the fold of Islam. For example: Abu Bakr (the tribe of Taym); Uthman ibn 'Affan (the tribe of Banu Umayyah); 'Ali ibn Abi Talib (the tribe of Banu Hashim); Zubayr ibn al-'Awwam (the tribe of Banu Asad); Mus'ab ibn 'Umayr (the tribe of Banu Abd al-Dar); 'Abdul Rahman ibn 'Awf (the tribe of Banu Zuhra); Sa'id ibn Zayd (the tribe of Banu 'Adi); Abdullah ibn Mas'ud (the tribe of Huzayl); Ammar ibn Yasir (the tribe of 'Ans), and Tufayl ibn 'Amr (the tribe of Daws).

In this way, the dawah work in Makkah began to take on a good shape. Meanwhile, the Quraysh had discovered that more and more people were following the Prophet. They were not happy with the mission of the Prophet, which was taking people away from their old tribal ways and they tried to stop it by creating obstacles and difficulties.

Once a year, during the period of Hajj, many people from all over Arabia would gather for the pilgrimage to Makkah. The Prophet Muhammad ﷺ would use this opportunity to meet people in

their gatherings and present Islam to them. He would read out portions of the Quran to enlighten them.

In the same way, the Prophet would go to the various fairs, such as Ukaz, Majnnah and Dhul Majaz. A lot of people came to the fairs to trade camels and everyday goods. Therefore, these were good occasions to meet more and more people and tell them about Islam.

Abdullah ibn Wabisah al-Abasi recounts that his father and grandfather were in Mina during the Hajj. The Prophet Muhammad ﷺ came to meet them in their tents.

This is what Abdullah ibn Wabisah al-Abasi had to say about the first meeting with the Prophet in his own words:

"We were staying near Khaif at the first stoning pillar when the Prophet came. He was mounted on his she-camel. Zayd ibn Haritha was sitting right behind him. The Prophet presented Islam to us and called us to accept Islam. None of us said a word in response to his call. The Prophet kept on preaching and we all stood listening to him without responding to him at all.

"Maysara ibn Masruq al-Abasi was also present among us. He was moved by the words of the Prophet. He said, "What the Prophet is saying makes a lot of sense to me. It would be great if we took him into the midst of our caravan."

His people answered, "Don't do this. No one is going to listen him."

When the Prophet heard the good and encouraging words, he said to Maysara, "Why don't you accept it?"

"There is no doubt, what you say sounds very good to me." Maysara replied, "But what can I do? If I accept your religion, my tribe will turn against me. A man can only live with his tribe."

Most of the people were thus set in their old ways and were scared to do without the backing of their own

tribes. In this way, no one paid any heed to the Prophet's call, and he returned from there disappointed.

One day, it so happened that the Prophet Muhammad ﷺ decided that the time had come to address the people in an open gathering. He stood atop the little hillock of Safa, near the Kabah, and spoke to the crowd gathered there.

It was an old tradition that if a person had something to announce, he would climb the hill of Safa and speak from there. A crowd would soon gather to hear to what he had to say.

In the same way, when the Prophet Muhammad ﷺ stood atop the hillock of Safa, a large crowd gathered to listen to him as he called out loudly, "Ya Sabaha."

He then asked, "O people of the Quraysh, if I told you that an army was advancing to attack you from the nearby hills, would you believe me?"

"Yes, we would surely believe you," answered the people, "We have always known you to be truthful."

Having heard their answer, the Prophet then called the different tribes by their name.

"O Banu Abdul Muttalib! O Banu Abd Manaf! O Banu Zuhrah! The way you sleep, you will die. The way you get up from sleep you will

be raised again after death. After that, either there is eternal paradise or eternal hell."

People remained silent on hearing these words.

The Prophet went on and told them, "Allah has made me the Last Prophet to mankind and revealed the Quran to me. We must worship one God and submit ourselves to His will. If you will not do so, you will be accountable on the Day of Judgement, and God will punish you."

Abu Lahab, who was one of the uncles of the Prophet, was also present among the crowd. He shouted in derision, "Was this all you called us here for?"

Then he said to the gathering, "Do not listen to a word of that he says. Go back to your homes. Muhammad has lost his mind."

The people, who held Abu Lahab in high esteem, as he was an important man in Makkah, started to disperse. After a while, only Ali ibn Abi Talib, who was just ten years old, and Zayd ibn Haritha remained there with the Prophet.

When the Prophet Muhammad ﷺ began his mission of dawah work – conveying the message of the Quran to the people at large. His own tribe, the Quraysh, refused to support him.

Rather, they began to mock him. When they saw that this had no effect on the Prophet and that he continued to carry on his work, they started to persecute him in the most terrible ways.

One day it happened that the Prophet was so badly injured by the stones thrown at him by the people of the Quraysh, that by the time he got back home he was bleeding. His family was appalled to see him in this state but he comforted them and said:

"Don't worry, it is nothing. The wounds will heal in no time."

However, the next day, the Prophet was in so much pain, due to the injuries on his face and body, that he could not go to the Kabah to pray. So the handful Muslims who had gathered in the Kabah to pray, performed their prayers without the Prophet. When these people prostrated themselves (*sajdah*), all of a sudden the people of the Quraysh tribe attacked them from behind. Many Muslims were seriously injured.

Abu Lahab and his wife were close relatives of the Prophet Muhammad ﷺ. In spite of that, they became his most violent enemies. They would throw stones at the Prophet's house and would incite street urchins to do the same. They would even throw dirt and the carcasses of dead animals at the Prophet's house but the Prophet would bear these insults with great patience.

Abu Lahab's wife, Jamila, went to such great

lengths to make the Prophet's life miserable that, she would spread thorns on the path along which the Prophet was to pass. Often sharp thorns would pierce the Prophet's feet, making it impossible for him to walk. When he reached his home, he would painstakingly remove the thorns, and blood would ooze from the wounds all over his feet. This made it difficult for him to walk for many days to come.

Moreover, not a single day passed without the Prophet returning from the Kabah with some part or the other of his body bleeding. The people of the Quraysh would injure him by cruelly throwing stones at him.

Sa'd ibn Abi Waqqas, an early Companion of the Prophet says:

"At that time, it was not possible for us Muslims to perform a congregational prayer at the Kabah. It was only possible to gather at some place other than the Kabah, as the Quraysh constantly kept a watch over us. If we gathered at the house of any Muslim, the Quraysh would immediately get to know about it and would attack us, inflicting serious injuries on us.

"For this reason, we would go out of Makkah and perform our prayers at some remote place. We kept shifting our place of prayer, as the Quraysh would get to know if we said our prayers at any one place on a regular basis. Even if it was outside Makkah in some remote valley, they

would follow us there and harass us."

The essence of the Prophet Muhammad's preaching was to tell people about the purpose of life: to explain the creation plan of the Almighty Allah, when He had created the universe. Also, the Prophet answered such questions as: What is life? What is death? What is the purpose for which man has been sent to earth? How should he conduct himself in this life?

How should he live in this world to be successful in the Hereafter?

In the early Makkan period, the Prophet received mostly the shorter chapters of the Quran, which dealt mainly with the Day of Judgement, Doomsday, Paradise and Hell.

The Prophet, therefore, would read out these passages of the Quran to people and then would explain to them that this life had been given to them, so that they could make themselves deserving candidates to enter Paradise.

He would explain that the key to enter Paradise was the purification of the soul – *tazkiyah*. This meant that one should banish from one's heart all kinds of negative feelings such as anger, revenge, violence, intolerance, arrogance and the like, and become completely positive in one's personality. Paradise would thus be given to those who were able to make themselves completely positive souls.

When the Prophet Muhammad ﷺ started preaching the Oneness of Allah, the people of Makkah understood that he was saying that the religion of polytheism they followed was baseless and wrong. Therefore, they turned against the Prophet. Thus began a period of extreme suffering for the Prophet and the handful of Muslims who followed him.

Once, at the request of Abu Bakr, the Prophet Muhammad ﷺ came to the Kabah. Seeing the Prophet there, a number of Muslims gathered at the Kabah. Abu Bakr stood up and started addressing the gathering. While Abu Bakr was giving his speech, some of the people of the Quraysh lost their temper. They rained blows on the Prophet and the other Muslims with all their might. Utbah ibn Rabia hit Abu Bakr so hard in the face that he started bleeding profusely. The Muslims were surrounded on

all sides and could not get away from their persecutors. After a short while the relatives of Abu Bakr arrived there and got him out of the clutches of the Quraysh with great difficulty.

Abu Dharr Ghifari was living far away from Makkah among the tribe of Ghifar. One day he heard that there was a man in Makkah who declared that he was the Messenger of God and that he received the revelations of the Quran from God.

Abu Dharr Ghifari was curious to know more about this person. He sent his elder brother, Unays Ghifari, to Makkah and asked him to find out the truth about this man who claimed to be the Prophet and said that he received revelations from Allah. He also asked him to listen to the revelations and give him his true opinion about the Prophet and his words.

Unays Ghifari took a camel and rode to Makkah. He met the Prophet Muhammad ﷺ and got a good idea about his teachings and message. Unays later left Makkah and arrived back his home.

Once home, Unays Ghifari went to his brother and told him, that he had met Muhammad ibn Abdullah. He found that in Makkah people called him "a liar", "a magician", "a poet" and "a soothsayer."

However, Unays was an intelligent person.

He was a poet as well. So he told his brother, "But I have heard many storytellers and Muhammad's speech was not like that of a storyteller, nor was what he said poetry. I swear to God, he is a truthful person."

Then Unays added, "I saw him preaching goodness and he stopped people from doing evil. He strongly urged people to have a good moral character."

After hearing the good things his brother had to say about the Prophet Muhammad ﷺ, Abu Dharr Ghifari became inspired to visit Makkah himself. So he prepared his camel. He took his water bag with drinking water and some food to keep him going on the long journey. Then he set out towards Makkah. After reaching Makkah

he first met Ali ibn Abi Talib, who took him to
the Prophet Muhammad ﷺ. Abu Dharr Ghifari
met the Prophet Muhammad ﷺ and listened
to what he had to say. Since Abu Dharr was a
truth seeker, it took him no time to convince
himself that the Quran was the word of God. He
immediately accepted Islam by reciting
the *shahadah*. After accepting Islam, Abu Dharr
Ghifari went to the Kabah. He said his prayers

there and openly announced his acceptance of Islam. The people of the Quraysh who were present there did not like this. They started beating him. They tortured him so much that Abu Dharr collapsed and fell to the ground. It was only when Al-Abbas came there that he managed to rescue him from his enemies.

Afterwards, the Prophet Muhammad ﷺ told him to go back to his tribe and introduce Islam to them. Then the Prophet added, "For some time, you should remain there and then when you feel that situation here has improved, you could return to me."

So Abu Dharr Ghifari returned to his clan. The first one to accept Islam was his elder brother, Unays Ghifari. Then both the brothers invited their mother to Islam. She too understood the truth in the teachings of Islam, so she also accepted Islam. In this way Abu Dharr Ghifari and his family began to do dawah work among his tribe and, due to their work, almost half of the Ghifari tribe accepted Islam in a few years' time.

اللَّهُمَّ افْتَحْ لِي اَبْوَابَ رَحْمَتِكَ.

O Allah, open for me the
doors of Your mercy.

"Part of being a good
Muslim is taking no
undue interest in what
does not concern one."

Tirmidhi

The
Early
Muslims

For almost three years, dawah activities were limited to individual meetings and private circles.

Later, there came a revelation of the Quran which commanded the Prophet Muhammad ﷺ

to perform dawah publicly: "Warn your close relatives."

So the Prophet Muhammad ﷺ invited people of his clan the Banu Hashim for a meal. The charge of organizing the meal was given to Ali ibn Abi Talib, who arranged milk and dates for the guests.

About forty men of the Banu Hashim assembled at the Prophet's house. After they had had their meal, the Prophet gave a brief speech.

He said, "I have come to you as a blessing for the world and the hereafter. I don't know if in all of Arabia anyone has brought a better thing than this. Tell me who will support me."

148

And then the Prophet added, "Whoever supports me, will be in Paradise with me."

Since the message of Islam had already reached most of the people, it was not difficult to understand what the Prophet said.

There was pin drop silence. No one said a single word. The Prophet repeated his words two or three times. But no one responded to his call.

Seeing this Ali ibn Abi Talib, who was about 12 year old, got up and said,

"Though I have pain in my eyes and my legs are weak, though I am the youngest of you all, O my brother, I will support you."

Seeing this the Prophet exclaimed, "You O Ali, You O Ali!" Meaning, you are merely a young boy, how can you help me and support me.

Also present at the gathering was Al-Abbas, the Prophet's uncle, who was a rich man. He could easily have made himself responsibile for the Prophet and supported him in his cause. But he too remained silent.

All the relatives who were assembled there got up and went away. No one showed any interest in helping or supporting the Prophet in his mission of dawah work.

The Quraysh wanted to stop the Prophet Muhammad ﷺ from spreading his new religion. They attacked him. They abused him. They tortured his Companions. They even killed some of them. But the Prophet did not react and continued his work with patience, as he had been commanded by Allah to convey the message of the Quran to others.

The Quraysh knew that since Abu Talib, the Prophet's uncle, was protecting him and helping in his work, so they came to meet Abu Talib. They told him to tell his nephew, Muhammad, to stop his activities.

Abu Talib called the Prophet Muhammad ﷺ and asked him to stop his mission as it would be very difficult for him to bear the enmity of the Quraysh.

The Prophet Muhammad ﷺ replied, "O Uncle! By God Almighty, even if they put the sun on my right hand and the moon on my left hand, I will not stop my work."

Seeing the firm commitment and zeal the Prophet showed by saying such fine words, Abu Talib was moved too. "Go forth, my nephew," assured Abu Talib, "and do what you want to do. I swear by God that I will never hand you over to your enemies."

In the tribal age, there were no police, no army and no government as we have today. So no person could survive without the support of his tribe. The Prophet belonged to the Banu Hashim. Due to Abu Talib's support for and protection of the Prophet Muhammad ﷺ,

the entire clan of the Banu Hashim came to the support of the Prophet Muhammad ﷺ.

One day the Prophet Muhammad ﷺ was praying on top of a hillock in Makkah. When Abu Jahl saw him praying, he took a stone in his hand and hit the Prophet with it. The Prophet got injured and started bleeding profusely. Seeing this a man rushed to Hamza and said, "O Hamza what has happened to your honour, Abu Jahl has hit your nephew very hard with a stone. Why don't you go and help him?"

Hamza was a very strong man, like a wrestler. He had just returned from a hunting trip. He had a bow in his hand made of iron.

Hearing this, Hamza got up in anger and went straight to Abu Jahl's house. He called him from outside the house. As soon as Abu Jahl came out of his house, Hamza hit Abu Jahl very hard with the iron bow he was carrying in his hand. The blow was so hard that Abu Jahl started bleeding from his head.

Afterwards Hamza came to the Prophet Muhammad ﷺ and told him, "Nephew, I have avenged you."

The Prophet calmly replied, "Uncle, I would have been happier if you had accepted Islam."

Hearing these words of the Prophet, Hamza lost no time in repeating the shahadah, and embracing Islam.

When Hamza came back home there were some people who condemned him, saying,

"You have left the religion of your forefathers. You have become irreligious." Due to this, Hamza became restless and thought that he had probably done something wrong. He could not sleep the whole night. The next morning he went to the Kabah and prayed to Allah, "O Allah, if the way of Muhammad is the right way, then implant the firmness of truth in my heart. Otherwise let me come out this state in which I find myself now. Open my heart to the truth and let my suspicion vanish."

Later he met the Prophet Muhammad ﷺ and told him what was going on in his heart.

The Prophet clarified his doubts and gave him the good

news of Paradise and warned him about Hellfire. After this his heart calmed down and his mind became easy about the truthfulness of the Prophet's message.

Hamza said to the Prophet, "I bear witness that you speak the truth."

"O my nephew," said Hamza, "I am going to announce that I have accepted Islam and will not give it up, even if I were given everything on which the sun rises."

Due to Hamza's accepting Islam, some other people also accepted Islam and the number of Muslims rose to thirty.

Once Abu Sufyan was going to his farm on horseback with his wife, Hind. His son Muawiyah, who was still quite young, was riding a donkey. Abu Sufyan saw the Prophet Muhammad ﷺ coming towards them. He told his son, Muawiyah, to get down from the donkey and let the Prophet ride it. Muawiyah got down and let the Prophet mount the donkey. The Prophet rode along with them for a while.

The Prophet then addressed them, saying, "O Sufyan ibn Harb and O Hind bint Utbah, I swear by God, you will surely die one day. You will be raised again after death. Then the righteous will go to Paradise and the wicked will go to Hell."

Muawiyah says that after telling them this, the Prophet got down from the donkey and went away. Then he remounted the donkey.

He says, my mother said to my father, "Was it for this magician that you got my son down from the donkey?" To which Abu Sufyan replied, "I swear by God, he is not a magician, he is not a liar."

Abu Jahl was one of the direst enemies of Islam and the Prophet Muhammad ﷺ. He had a maid whose name was Sumayyah. Abu Jahl had bought her as a slave.

When the teachings of the Prophet Muhammad ﷺ spread in Makkah, Sumayyah also became influenced by them and accepted Islam.

When Abu Jahl came to know about Sumayyah's acceptance of Islam, he became furious. He said to Sumayyah, "You must abandon this new faith." "I will not leave

Muhammad's religion," said Sumayyah firmly.

This made Abu Jahl even more furious. He took some ropes and tied her to a pole. He flogged her so much that she fainted.

In those days slaves had no rights. Since Sumayyah was a slave no one could come to her rescue.

When Abu Bakr came to know about it, he decided to meet Abu Jahl and set her free by handing over some money. He had already bought six slaves who had accepted Islam and set them free. He came to Abu Jahl and offered one hundred dirhams to sell Sumayyah to him, so that he could set her free. Abu Jahl did not agree to this, so he offered one hundred and fifty dirhams.

But Abu Jahl did not agree to his offer. Then Abu Bakr said, "Tell me what amount you need, and I will pay it." But Abu Jahl would not agree to sell Sumayyah at any cost.

Sumayyah worked as a midwife too. So many women of the Quraysh whom Sumayyah had helped in child birth, came and pleaded with Abu Jahl not to torture Sumayyah any more. But he did not listen to anyone. Abu Jahl flogged Sumayyah so much that her entire body was covered with deep wounds and blood started flowing from everywhere. Though she was almost fainting, she kept repeating, "I will not leave Muhammad's religion."

At last when Sumayyah would not listen to Abu Jahl, he took her one day near to the Kabah and asked in front of all the people, "Will you leave the religion of Muhammad or not?"

Sumayyah said, "No", to this. Abu Jahl became red with anger and hit her so hard with the spear in his hands that Sumayyah died on the spot.

Thus Sumayyah became the first martyr of Islam.

There were two people in Makkah who were distinguished for their unmatched leadership qualities. They were Umar ibn al-Khattab and Amr ibn Hisham, who was also known as Abu Jahl.

The Prophet Muhammad ﷺ once prayed, "O Allah, give support to Islam through one of these two Umars." The Prophet's prayer was answered and after some time Umar ibn al-Khattab embraced Islam.

'Umar ibn al-Khattab was an important man of Makkah. He was rich. He was very brave. And he was also very stubborn.

'Umar refused to accept Islam. He troubled the Muslims. He did not let them pray in peace. And he threatened to beat anybody who opposed him. People were very afraid of him. One day the Prophet and his followers gathered in a house to pray. 'Umar came to know about it. Sword in hand, he rushed towards the house. A man saw him walking in haste and asked him: "Where are you going with a sword in your hand?" 'Umar said: "I am going to kill Muhammad. He is spreading mischief among our people."

The man said to 'Umar: "If you kill Muhammad, his tribe will kill you. Let him be. It would be better if you saw what is happening in your own family." "What is the matter with my family?" asked 'Umar. The man answered: "Your sister and her husband have become Muslims. And you know nothing about it!"

'Umar turned around and ran to his sister's house. He stopped outside the door and listened. He could hear somebody reading aloud. He pushed the door open and went in.

'Umar's sister hid the paper from which they were reading. Seeing this, 'Umar became so angry that he hit his sister. Then he hit his brother-in-law.

He said: "Have you become Muslims?" They were afraid of 'Umar but loved Allah best. They said: "Yes. We are Muslims. We believe in Allah and His Prophet. Do what you like."

When 'Umar saw that he had hurt his sister, he became ashamed. He said to her: "Give me that paper. Let me read what is written there."

She handed him over the paper on which, Surah Ta Ha was written. He started reading it.

When he reached verse 14, "I am Allah. There is no deity save Me; so worship Me alone, and say your prayers in My remembrance", he felt as if these verses were addressed to him in person and Allah was talking to him. He immediately decided not to lose any more time in following the truth. He turned to his sister and brother-in-law and said, "I came to you as an enemy of Islam; I go from you as a friend of Islam. I buckled on this sword to slay the Prophet of Islam; I now go to him to offer my allegiance." Fatima and Sa'id called out, "*Allahu Akbar!*" (God is great!)

'Umar turned around and went to meet the Prophet Muhammad ﷺ. He said to him: "O Messenger of Allah, I have come to tell you that I believe in Allah." The Prophet embraced him. Thus Islam was strengthen by 'Umar ibn al-Khattab becoming a Muslim.

Amr ibn Abasa was a truth seeker. He was not content with the religion of his forefathers. So one day he came to know about the Prophet Muhammad ﷺ. Riding a she-camel, he reached Makkah and met the Prophet Muhammad ﷺ. He came to know the people of his tribe were against him, and so, the Prophet was doing his work in secret. After searching for a while, he finally reached the place where the Prophet Muhammad ﷺ was staying. Amr ibn Abasa asked, "Who are you?" "I am the Prophet of God," said the Prophet Muhammad ﷺ.

"What is the meaning of Prophet?" asked Amr ibn Abasa. "The Prophet is a person who brings a message from Allah," replied the Prophet.

"Is it true that Allah has sent you?" asked Amr ibn Abasa.

"Yes," said the Prophet.

"To worship One God, and not to associate anyone with Him, and to be kind to relatives and kinsmen," continued the Prophet.

"Who are helping you in this work?" asked Amr ibn Abasa.

"A freeman and a slave," said the Prophet Muhammad ﷺ, meaning Abu Bakr and Bilal.

Then Amr ibn Abasa said, "I want to be with you in your mission."

The Prophet said to him that this was not the right time for him to be there and to become a part of this mission. He told him to return to his village and when he heard favourable news about him, then he should come back.

So Amr ibn Abasa accepted Islam and returned to his home.

Zimad belonged to the tribe of Azdshanoh. Once he came to Makkah on a pilgrimage. At one place he saw Abu Jahl, Utbah ibn Rabia and Umayyah ibn Khalf talking to each other. Zimad also sat with them. Abu Jahl said, "This man (meaning the Prophet Muhammad ﷺ) has brought discord to our groups. He thinks our pious ancestors were all misguided." To this Umayyah said, "He must be a madman."

On hearing this, Zimad thought that probably the Prophet Muhammad had been possessed by some evil spirit. Since he used to cure such people who were possessed by evil spirits, he set out to meet him. He searched for him the whole day, but could not find him. The next day he found the Prophet praying at Maqam Ibrahim near the Kabah. When the Prophet had finished his prayers, Zimad approached him and said, "O Muhammad I cure these things. If you let me do this for you, hopefully, God will give you a cure and good health."

To this the Prophet Muhammad ﷺ did not respond. The Prophet said, "All praise is due to Allah, we seek help from Him alone. To whom Allah shows the right path, no one can misguide him. And to whom He misguides, no one can bring him to the right path."

The Prophet further said, "I bear witness that only Allah is worth worshipping. No one is His partner." The Prophet said this three times.

Zimad was quite mesmerized by these beautiful words from the Prophet. So he thought that he had heard the

171

storytellers, the magicians and the poets, but what the Prophet said he had never heard in his whole life.

The Prophet extended his hands to Zimad. He took his hands right there and then entered the fold of Islam.

Haseen was an old man. He was very respected among the Quraysh tribe. One day some of the members of the Quraysh tribe came to him and said, "Please talk to this man (the Prophet Muhammad ﷺ). He offends our deities."

Haseen agreed to do so and accompanied them to meet the Prophet Muhammad ﷺ.

Haseen said, "I have heard that you offend our deities,

though your father was a very good man."
The Prophet asked Haseen, "How many
deities do you worship?"

To which Haseen said, "Seven deities
on the earth and one in heaven."

The Prophet asked, "When you are
in distress, to which deity do you call for
help?" "To the one in the heaven," said
Haseen.

The Prophet asked him again, "When
you suffer some loss in your wealth, to
whom do you call for help?" "To the one in
the heaven," replied Haseen.

The Prophet said to him that the God
who listened to his distress is One. But he
associated other gods with him.

Haseen thought that he had never spoken to such a person in his whole life.

Afterwards the Prophet Muhammad ﷺ told Haseen, "Accept Islam, you will be successful in the Hereafter."

Haseen said, "What should I say about my family and children?"

Then the Prophet Muhammad ﷺ taught him a beautiful prayer: "O Allah, I am a seeker of guidance from You. Please correct my affairs, and give me such knowledge as gives me benefit."

Haseen repeated this prayer and accepted the faith before leaving that place.

A delegation of the Khazraj tribe came to Makkah from Madinah. They were visiting Makkah to make some agreement with the

Quraysh tribe. One of the members of the delegation was Iyas ibn Mu'adh.

When the Prophet Muhammad ﷺ came to know about this delegation, he went to meet them.

The Prophet sat with them and said, "Should I tell you something better than that for which you have come here?"

"What is that?" they asked.

The Prophet said, "I am the Prophet sent by Allah. Allah has sent me to His servants, so that I may call people to Allah and tell them that they should  worship Allah alone, and not associate anyone with Him. Allah has sent down His book to me."

Then the Prophet read some verses from the Quran to them.

Iyas ibn Mu'adh was a young man at that time. When he heard the Prophet, he said to his people, "O my people, I swear to God, this is surely better than that for which you have come here."

Hearing these words from Ibn Mu'adh, Anas ibn Rafay took some dust in his hands and threw it in the face of Ibn Mu'adh, and said, "Leave these things, we have come here for some other purpose." Seeing his anger at and disapproval of the Prophet, Ibn Mu'adh became silent.

Later the Prophet Muhammad ﷺ went away and the people in the delegation left Makkah after completing their work.

Soon after reaching Madinah, Ibn Mu'adh
fell ill and passed away. One of the people of his
tribe, who was present at the time of his death,
said, "Ibn Mu'adh was repeating the words,
'La ilaha illallah Allahu Akbar wa Subhan Allah.'"
Meaning there is no deity other than Allah.
God is Great and Glory be to God.

In those days of tribal rules, no one could live
without the support of his tribe. After the death

of the Prophet's uncle, whose name was Abu Talib, the Prophet lost his biggest supporter and helper.

Now the tribe of the Quraysh became more violent and aggressive in torturing the Muslims and making life difficult for the Prophet Muhammad ﷺ.

During the Hajj season, the Prophet Muhamamd ﷺ would visit the fairs of Ukaz, Majannah and Dhul Majaz and also visit people at their homes and present Islam to them. He also asked people to give him their protection, so that he could carry out his prophetic mission. He would tell them that whoever helped him in this task would be rewarded with Paradise. Not a single tribe agreed to protect the Prophet

Muhammad ﷺ or help him. He went to each and
every tribe of Arabia one by one, but none of
them agreed to help him or protect him.

He went to the tribe of the Banu Amir ibn
Sa'sa'ah. They treated the Prophet very badly.
They turned him away, throwing stones at him.

The Prophet went to see the people of the
tribe of Banu Muharib ibn Khasfa. There was an
old man who was a hundred years of age.

The Prophet Muhammad ﷺ told him about
the Oneness of Allah (*tawheed*) and asked him

to take him under his
protection, so that he
could convey the message
of Allah to the people.
The old man replied, "Your

tribe knows you better. I swear to God that whoever takes you from here to his place, will be the worst man to take home anything from here on the season of Hajj. Therefore, please excuse me."

Maysarah ibn Masruq, who was among them, said to the people of their tribe, "I swear to God, if we obey this man and take him to our tribe, it will surely be a good thing for us. I swear to God this man's words will dominate that it will reach everywhere."

Hearing Maysarah, the people of his tribe said, "Leave it, why do you say something which none of us is going to accept?"

When the Prophet heard Maysarah, he became hopeful about him. He said to Maysarah,

"Why you yourself do not accept this message."
"What you are saying seems very pleasant to me,"
said Maysarah, "but if I accept what you say, my
tribe will go against me. And you know that no
man can live without the support of his tribe."

رَبِّ اجْعَلْنِي لَكَ شَكَّاراً، لَكَ
ذَكَّاراً، لَكَ رَهَّاباً، لَكَ مِطْوَاعاً،
لَكَ مُخْبِتاً، اِلَيْكَ اَوَّاهاً مُنِيْباً.

My Lord, cause me to thank You,
to remember You, to fear You, to
obey You, to humble myself before
You, to turn toward You tearfully
and penitently.

"On the Day of Resurrection, Allah will not look at the person who trails his robe behind him out of pride."

Bukhari and Muslim

The
Helplessness
of the Quraysh

As the Prophet carried on with his mission in Makkah, slowly, people began to accept Islam. Some of them were already giving up the worship of idols and other deities, and

when they heard the message of the oneness
of God (or what in Islam is called *tawheed*),
they immediately felt that this was the Truth.
And so, they became believers in Islam. The
early converts included the wife of the Prophet,
Khadija; his childhood friend, Abu Bakr;
his cousin, Ali ibn Abi Talib; and Umar Ibn
Khattab, who had once been a dire enemy of the
Prophet. All these people took up the dawah
mission of the Prophet seriously and played an
important role in spreading the message of Islam.

Others heard from Christian and Jewish
priests and scholars on their visits to Syria and
Palestine that a prophet would soon appear in
Arabia. When they saw the Prophet Muhammad ﷺ,
they were impressed by his noble character and

his message, and so they entered the fold
of Islam.

One person dreamt that the Prophet
Muhammad ﷺ was pulling him out of a pit of
fire. He met the Prophet, heard some of the
verses of the Quran from him, and then testified
to the truth of Islam and accepted the faith.

One of those who accepted at this time was
Uthman ibn Affan.

Uthman ibn Affan was born around 576 A.D.,
in a town called Taif in Arabia.

He was about six years younger than the Prophet Muhammad ﷺ. Both his parents were distant relatives of the Prophet. Uthman, having received a formal education, he was one of the few people in those times in Makkah who could read and write. Uthman was one of the most prosperous and well-known men of Makkah. He had inherited a great deal of wealth from his father. Like his father, he became a merchant. His straight-forwardness and business skills soon made him one of the richest men among the Quraysh, the tribe to which the Prophet, too, belonged. Soon, he came to be known as Uthman Ghani or 'Uthman the Rich'.

Uthman was known for his modesty and good character. Even before becoming a Muslim, he never gambled or drank wine. He led a simple life. Whenever he could, he helped widows, orphans and the poor. He was kind to his relatives.

One day, Uthman visited his aunt Arwah, as she was unwell. The Prophet Muhammad ﷺ was there, too. Uthman started looking at the Prophet curiously, as people were talking a lot about him. Noticing this, the Prophet asked, "Uthman, what is the matter?"

Uthman replied, "I am surprised to see that we once honoured you and held you in great esteem. But what is happening now?"

Uthman was referring to
the fact that the Quraysh
were now opposed to the
Prophet because of his
religious mission.

In reply to this, the Prophet
recited some verses of the Quran.

Uthman was so impressed by what he heard
that he went along with the Prophet to the
Prophet's house and there he accepted Islam.

In the early period of his mission, this was
how people were attracted to the Prophet. In
this way, people from Makkah entered the fold
of Islam.

Slowly, but steadily, Islam started spreading
in Makkan homes. Everywhere, people started

talking about it. According to Ibn Ishaq, the earliest biographer of the Prophet, the Prophet conveyed the message of Islam to people, one by one, on an individual basis, for three years. Later, when Surah al-Muddaththir was revealed, the Prophet was commanded by Allah to warn people publicly. This is how the Quran puts it: "O you, wrapped up in your cloak, arise and give warning."

The Makkans now started opposing the Prophet's mission openly. Their hostility and persecution went on growing. But God instructed the Prophet to bear all this patiently. And so, he and his Companions would go out of Makkah and pray secretly, in some remote place outside the town.

The leaders of the Quraysh tribe were very unhappy to see the Prophet's mission spread in Makkah. The major reason for this was that the Prophet objected to their religious beliefs and ways of worship. Basically, it was a rift between *shirk*, or associating others with God, and *tawheed*, the worship of the one God. However, they could not harm the Prophet, as Abu Talib, the Prophet's uncle who had raised him after the death of his father and grandfather, protected him.

In those days in Arabia, if a tribe protected someone, to harm him would mean quarrelling with the entire tribe.

So, the leaders of the Quraysh came to Abu Talib to talk to him about the Prophet. They told Abu Talib that his nephew, Muhammad, condemned their deities and that he had said that their forefathers had been ignorant, because they blindly followed the beliefs and ways of their ancestors, not using their reason to consider whether these beliefs were right or wrong. They insisted that Abu Talib should stop the Prophet from doing this. Otherwise,

they said, he should let them deal with him themselves. They wanted Abu Talib to cease giving protection to the Prophet, so that the Quraysh could have a free hand to forcibly stop the Prophet's mission.

Abu Talib patiently heard the men out, and then let them return. He refused to do as the leaders of the Quraysh wanted him to.

And so, the Prophet continued his mission with Abu Talib's support.

After some time, the leaders of the Quraysh came to meet Abu Talib again.

They said to him, "We have great respect for you, because you are a wise man and one of our elders. We asked you to stop your nephew Muhammad, but you did not. We swear to God we will not be patient if he goes on condemning our ancestors and saying bad things about our deities. Either you stop him now or we will wage war against him. We expect that you will not interfere in this."

Having said this, they went away.

Abu Talib felt very bad about his fellow tribesmen turning into his enemies. But, at the same time, he did not want to hand over the Prophet to them or to leave him without his support.

Abu Talib called the Prophet and said, "The leaders of our tribe came to me and they said many things to me. Now, please be merciful to me, and to yourself, too. Do not make me have to face so much trouble that I won't be able to bear it." The Prophet thought that his uncle had changed his stand and that he would stop protecting and supporting him.

He said, "O my uncle! Even if they put the sun in my right hand and the moon in my left, I will not stop my work till Allah brings success to this mission or I die for its cause."

Saying this, tears came to his eyes. He got up and started to leave Abu Talib's house. Abu Talib called out to him, "Nephew, come here!"

Abu Talib then said to him, "O my nephew, go and say whatever you want to say. I swear to Allah that I will never hand you over to them, come what may."

The Prophet heaved a sigh of relief. He continued his work of dawah, of inviting people to tread God's path, as before. The Quraysh now realized that Abu Talib would

not stop protecting the Prophet. And so, their leaders went to see Abu Talib once again. They were accompanied by a man called Ammarah ibn al-Walid.

They said to Abu Talib, "This is Ammarah ibn al-Walid. He is the most handsome and the wealthiest person among us. You can keep him with you and treat him like your own son. In return, hand over your nephew Muhammad to us, so that we can kill him."

Abu Talib was horrified at this offer. He said, "What! I swear by God, this is such a wicked thing you are suggesting to me! Are you giving me your son, so that on your behalf I may feed him, while I give you my son so that you may kill him?"

"I swear by God!" said Abu Talib angrily, "This will never happen!"

One of the leaders of the Quraysh, Mut'im ibn Adi, spoke. "Our tribe has made a just suggestion," he said. "But you do not approve of it. It seems that you do not want to accept anything offered by your tribe!"

"I swear by God!" replied Abu Talib, "The Quraysh have not done me justice. You have firmly decided to go against me. So, go and do whatever you want!"

Seeing the hostile attitude of the Quraysh towards the Prophet, Abu Talib called on the Banu Hashim, the clan from among the Quraysh to which the Prophet belonged,

to defend the Prophet from the evil intentions of the Quraysh. Abu Talib encouraged them to support the Prophet. And so, the entire Banu Hashim clan rallied to the Prophet and gave him their full support and protection.

There was only one exception to this, though—a man called Abu Lahab. He was one of the Prophet's uncles. He refused to support the Prophet.

The leaders of the Quraysh then approached Walid ibn al-Mughirah, one of the most senior men in Makkah.

The season of Hajj was not far away.

Walid said to them, "The time of Hajj is very near. Many Arabs will start coming to Makkah for Hajj." He told them that people in different parts of Arabia had already come to hear about the Prophet. And so, he suggested, "You should come to some agreement among yourselves about him. It should not happen that you start talking differently in front of the people who will be coming for Hajj from different places, and in this way contradict one another."

The leaders of the Quraysh said to him, "Why don't you give us your opinion? We will accept it."

"No," replied Walid, "You speak, and I will listen."

The leaders of the Quraysh then said, "We will say that Muhammad is a soothsayer!" A soothsayer is a person who claims to see into the future. In ancient times, they were much in demand. People used to visit them in the hope of getting to know about what was going to happen to them.

Walid remarked, "No, I swear to God! I have seen soothsayers, and he is not a soothsayer!"

The Prophet did not speak like a soothsayer, he explained.

The leaders of the Quraysh said, "Then we will say that he is a madman!"

Walid said, "No, he is not a madman! I have seen mad people and I know what they are like!"

The Prophet was definitely not like them, he insisted.

The leaders of the Quraysh then said, "All right, we will say that he is a poet!"

To this Walid replied, "But he is not a poet either!"

Walid said that he knew various types of poetry, and he was sure that the Prophet's speech was not poetry.

They said, "Very well, then, we will call him a magician!"

To this, Walid replied, "He is not a magician! I have seen magicians, and he does not do any of the tricks that magicians perform!"

The leaders of the Quraysh were now in a fix.

Finally, they said, "Then you tell us what we should call him!"

"I swear by God!" Walid replied, "He speaks very kindly. The most you could say is that he is a magician. He talks in such a magical way that he creates discord between father and son; between brother and brother; between husband and wife and their families!"

The elders of the Quraysh agreed to Walid's suggestion. And then they left for their homes.

As people from different parts of Arabia started coming to Makkah during the Hajj season, the Quraysh sat by the wayside to mislead them about the Prophet. They tried to instigate them against him by saying false things about him.

When the people who had come for Hajj went back to their homes, they returned with news about the Prophet. In this way, all over Arabia people began to learn about the Prophet. The religion that the Prophet was preaching was earlier known only to the people of Makkah. But now all of Arabia came to know about it.

In those days, one of the ways to execute a criminal was to throw an animal's intestines on his head so that he died of suffocation and pain.

Once, the Prophet was praying at the Kabah. Abu Jahl, who was one of the chiefs of the Quraysh and leader of the Prophet's opponents, threw the foul-smelling intestines of a camel on the Prophet while he was prostrating himself in worship. The mess landed on his head and shoulders. Abu Jahl took one end of the intestines in his hands and tied up the other end around the Prophet's neck. The Prophet tried very hard to remove the intestines, but he could not. He was in great pain and distress, and unable to breathe properly.

No one came forward to help the Prophet. People were just too scared of Abu Jahl.

Seeing the Prophet in such a helpless state, a woman rushed to his home, which was located nearby. She told his daughter Ruqayyah about what she had seen.

Ruqayyah ran to the Kabah crying and found her father fighting for his life.

Abu Jahl and his allies stood around, laughing and joking. When they saw Ruqayyah approach, they moved aside.

Ruqayyah quickly untied the intestines, dragged the smelly mess from off the Prophet's head and wiped and cleaned his face and head with the edge of her robe.

The Prophet lay there in an almost unconscious condition for about an hour. Gradually, he recovered and got up with

Ruqayyah's help. He put his hand on Ruqayyah's shoulder and slowly walked towards his house.

The next day, the Prophet again went to the Kabah, as if nothing had happened to him the day before.

When the Quraysh saw the Prophet's determination, they devised another plan.

One day, when the Prophet was praying in front of the Kabah, a man named Utbah slowly entered the Kabah. He had some sheets of cloth in his hand. He was barefoot, and so he did not make any sound. He slowly tiptoed to where the Prophet was praying.

The moment the Prophet touched his head to the ground in prostration, Utbah flung the sheets over his head. Then, he started hitting the Prophet so hard that blood started oozing out from his face and nose.

After a brief struggle, the Prophet managed to set himself free from Utbah's clutches. Finally, he returned home, badly bleeding.

In this way, the Quraysh tried their best to stop the Prophet from spreading God's message. But all these hardships could not make him abandon his dawah work.

When the Quraysh saw that there was no way to stop the Prophet from carrying on with his mission, they met with a man called Utbah ibn Rabiah, who was considered one of the most distinguished leaders in Arabia. They requested him to meet the Prophet and make him some offers in a bid to stop his dawah work. They hoped that the Prophet would accept one of these offers, and, in return, would stop his mission. Utbah came to the Prophet and said, "O nephew! Are you better or your father, Abdullah?"

The Prophet kept quiet.

Utbah asked, "Are you better or your grandfather, Abd al-Muttalib?"

Again, the Prophet remained silent.

Utbah continued, "If you claim that your father and grandfather were better than you, they worshipped the same deities that you criticise! And if you say that you are better than them, we would certainly want to know what you have to say! You have caused discord among the people and have said bad things about our religion!"

After a while, Utbah said, "Listen carefully! I am going to make you some offers.

"If you are in need of wealth," Utbah explained, "We will give you so much wealth

that you will become the richest man of all the Quraysh. If you are afflicted by some disease, we will spend our wealth to cure you. If you want to marry, we will get you married to any of the Quraysh women. And if you want to be a king, we will crown you king over us!"

When Utbah stopped, the Prophet recited

Surah Fussilat, which is the forty-first chapter of the Quran.

Utbah listened attentively to the divine revelation. Facing him was a man who was devoid

of all ambitions of wealth, prestige, honour and power. He was indeed a man telling the truth, calling people to be good and to do good.

Utbah was spellbound by the beauty of the touching words of the Quran. He got up and quietly returned to his home. He stayed inside his house and did not go to the Quraysh to inform them about the outcome of his meeting with the Prophet. When Abu Jahl came to know about this, he said to the Quraysh, "Utbah has probably inclined towards Muhammad!"

Accompanied by his friends, Abu Jahl then went to Utbah's house and said to him, "I think you are inclined towards Muhammad."

Utbah remarked, "The reply which Muhammad gave me was neither poetry nor magic. It was not a cooked-up story either. Never in my whole life have I heard such a thing before! I was speechless! I did not know what to say! You are well aware that Muhammad does not tell lies. I fear that some punishment may befall you from the sky!"

After some time, the Quraysh approached the Prophet again. They said, "You very well know that we are deprived of natural resources. We do not have water. So, pray to the Lord who has sent you as a prophet to remove these mountains, because of which we are deprived of rain. Pray to your Lord to make our land spacious for us. And pray to your Lord to make rivers flow here, like those in Syria and Iraq!"

They added, "Pray to your Lord that He brings our elders back to life who have passed away. Bring Qusayy ibn Kilab back to life, as he was our elder and a truthful man. Then we will ask him if what you say is the truth or not. In this way, we will come to know whether you are a true prophet of God."

The Prophet replied, "I have not been sent to you for all this. I have come to you with the thing that Allah has given me."

By this he meant the Quran.

The Prophet continued, "And what Allah has given me, I have delivered it to you. If you accept it, you will have a share of His blessings in this world and in the Hereafter. And if you

reject it, let us wait for the command of Allah to come. Let us see what His decision is about me and about you."

The Quraysh replied, "If you are not ready to do for us what we have requested, then do it for yourself. Pray to your Lord," they said, "to send an angel to you, who will testify that what you say is true."

"Ask your Lord," they demanded, "to give you gardens, palaces and treasures of silver and gold, so that He sets you free from the work that we see you do. We see you going to markets, in the same way as we do. We also see you going about earning your living, like we do."

If the Prophet asked God for all these comforts and God granted his request, they said, they would believe his claim of being God's Prophet.

"I am not going to do any such thing," replied the Prophet. "Nor I am a person who would ask such things from my Lord."

"Allah has sent me," the Prophet explained, "as a plain warner and a bearer of good news. If you accept that with which I have been sent, you will have a reward in this world as well as in the Hereafter."

The Quraysh remarked, "Then do one thing. Why don't you let a piece of the sky fall on us?"

"We will not believe in you until you do so."

The Prophet said to them, "This is up to Allah. If it is His will to do this for you, He will surely do it."

The Quraysh said, "We swear to God, we are not going to believe in the Merciful. We will not spare you until we are destroyed or we destroy you."

When they said such things, the Prophet got up to leave. Abdullah ibn Abi Umayya also got up with him. He was the son of the Prophet's aunt, Atika bint Abdul Muttalib. Abdullah said to the Prophet, "By God, I am never going to believe in you unless you bring a staircase which goes up to the sky.

Then, you climb up it and reach the seven heavens. Then, you bring a book from there.

And then, four angels must accompany you to testify to your truthfulness."

Afterwards, the Prophet returned to his house very sad. He had gone to his tribe full of hope. But they had gone even further away from him.

أُعِيْذُكُمَا بِكَلِمَاتِ اللهِ التَّامَّةِ مِنْ كُلِّ شَيْطَانٍ وَهَامَّةٍ وَمِنْ كُلِّ عَيْنٍ لاَمَّةٍ.

I seek refuge for you in the perfect words of Allah from every satan, every harmful creature and from every evil eye.

"The most honorable of you is the one who is the most pious of you."

Bukhari and Muslim

The *Christian King Helps Out*

Despite the hatred of the leaders of Makkah for the Prophet, Islam was spreading rapidly in Makkah. Every day, someone or the other entered the fold of Islam. Seeing this, the leaders of Makkah were enraged. They began tormenting the Prophet's Companions.

At this point, the Prophet told his Companions to leave Makkah and shift elsewhere.

They asked him, "Where should we go, O Prophet of Allah?"

The Prophet said that they should go to Ethiopia, which was also known as Habsha. It was also called Abyssinia. It is a country in north-eastern Africa, separated from Arabia by the Red Sea.

In Ethiopia, the Prophet told them, there was a Christian king who was upright and just. In his kingdom, no one could oppress anyone else.

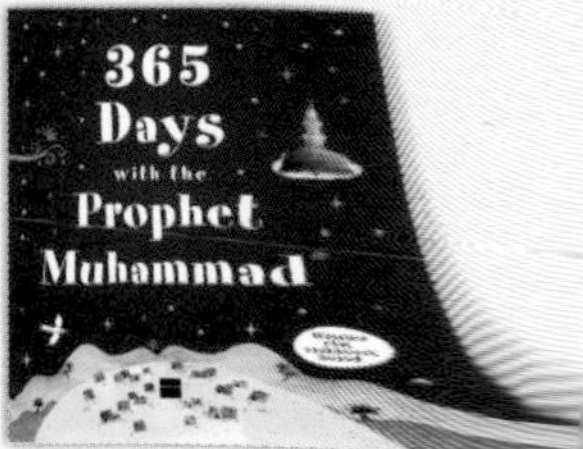

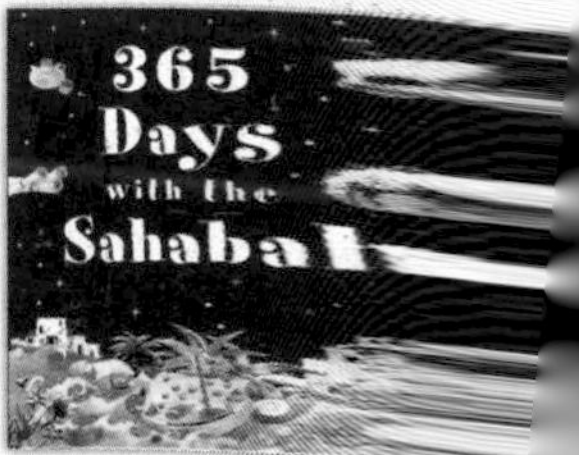

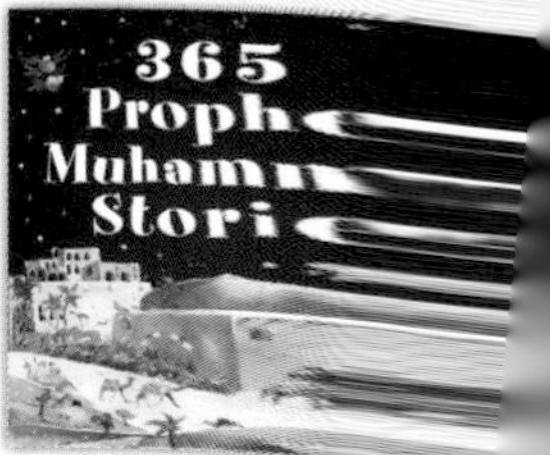

Good

And so, the Companions started moving out of Makkah and shifting to Ethiopia. This took place in the fifth year after the beginning of the revelation of the Quran.

The first group of Muslims who left Makkah for Ethiopia consisted of 11 men and five women. The group included Uthman ibn Affan and his wife, Ruqayyah, a daughter of the Prophet. They left Makkah secretly and finally reached the nearby seaport of Jeddah. In Jeddah, they found two ferries ready to leave for Ethiopia. They boarded the ferries, paying a sum of five dirhams each.

When the Makkans came to know about their escape, they sent

their men on horses to arrest them. But when they arrived at the port of Jeddah, the ferries had already set sail with the Muslims for Ethiopia!

Soon, this group of Muslims arrived in Ethiopia.

Shortly after, another, bigger, group of Muslims left Makkah for Ethiopia. This group consisted of 86 men and 17 women. Some of the

names of the Companions in this group are as follows:

1. Abu Hudhyfa ibn Utbah, and his wife Sahla bint Suhayl
2. Zubayr ibn al-Awwam
3. Musab ibn Umayr
4. Abdul Rahman ibn Awf
5. Abu Salama ibn Abdul Asad, and his wife Umm Salma bint Abu Umayya
6. Uthman ibn Mazun
7. Amir ibn Rabia
8. Abu Sabra ibn Abu Rahm
9. Suhayl ibn Bayda

When the Quraysh came to know that a large number of Muslims had migrated to Ethiopia and that they were living peacefully there, they consulted each other as to what to do about this. Finally, they decided to send Amr ibn al-As and Abdullalh ibn Abi Rabia with gifts for the Negus, the King of Ethiopia, and his courtiers in order to win their favour.

So Amr ibn al-As and Abdullah ibn Abi Rabia travelled to Ethiopia. They reached the Negus' palace and presented the gifts to his courtiers. They did this so that the courtiers would speak in their favour to the King. They told the courtiers that some simpletons from their town had arrived in their country. These men, they said, had abandoned the religion of their forefathers. They followed neither their forefathers' religion nor the religion of the Negus—that is to say, Christianity. They had, so they told the courtiers, devised a new religion, which neither they nor the Ethiopians knew anything of. Their tribe had sent them to Ethiopia so that they might take them back to their country.

They said, "Please help us by recommending us to the King so that he may hand them over to us."

The courtiers agreed to do so.

Amr ibn al-As and Abdullah ibn Abi Rabia came to meet the King in his palace. They prostrated themselves, in the customary manner, before the King. They presented him with gifts. Then, they told him that some of their people had changed their religion and had fled to his country. The people of Makkah had sent them to Ethiopia so that they could take them back to Makkah with them.

The King's courtiers also pleaded their case and advised the King to hand over the Muslims to them.

Amr ibn al-As and Abdullah ibn Abi Rabia wanted the King to hand the Muslims over to them without calling the Muslims to the court and hearing their side of the story.

But when they suggested this to the King, he was furious! He said, "I will never decide about them without talking to them."

Then, he ordered one of his men to bring the Muslims to his court. When the Muslims came to know about what had happened, they consulted each other about what to do. They agreed that they would say to the King what the Prophet Muhammad ﷺ had taught them.

They appeared in the King's court, where they greeted the King. However, they did not follow the custom of prostrating themselves before him. When asked why, Jafar ibn Abi Talib said, "We only prostrate ourselves before God. Our Prophet has taught us this."

Jafar ibn Abi Talib was the elder brother of Ali ibn Abi

Talib. The two were cousins of the Prophet Muhammad ﷺ. Jafar was a good speaker. And so, he represented the Muslims in the court of the Negus, the King of Ethiopia.

When the Negus inquired about their religion, Jafar replied: "O King! We were ignorant and sinful. We worshipped idols and ate animals which had not been sacrificed in the name of God. We did all kinds of bad things. We paid no respect to our relatives. We didn't help our neighbours. The strong among us took advantage of the weak. Then, a prophet—from amongst our own people, whose family history, honesty, fidelity and purity were well-known—

was sent to us by God. He called on us to stop worshipping the deities that our ancestors used to worship, and, instead, to worship the one God. He told us always to be truthful, to honour trusts, to fulfil our promises, to help neighbours and relatives, and to avoid all that is forbidden."

"He told us not to lie or bear false witness," Jafar continued. "He told us not to steal from orphans."

"He commanded us to bow to God alone, attributing no partners to Him," he added. "He told us to say our prayers regularly, to fast and to give zakat. We trusted his word and accepted his message from God. We followed him in both what he told us to do and what he told us to stay away from. Our own people tried, however, to turn us away from our religion. They caused us great grief and suffering in trying make us return to the sinful ways of earlier times."

"Because they treated us unjustly and made life unbearable for us in Makkah," Jafar explained, "we decided to come to your country. We came here in the hope that we might be protected, shown justice and be able to live in peace."

The King then asked Jafar, "Will you show me some of the revelations which your Prophet claims to have come to him from God?"

Jafar answered, "Yes!"

Then, he recited to him Chapter 19 of the Quran, which is known as Surah Maryam (or 'Mary'), from the beginning of the chapter till the following lines: "She [Mary] pointed to the child. They said, 'How shall we talk to someone who is a child in the cradle?' (But) he said, 'I am God's servant. He has given me the Book and made me a prophet; He has made me blessed wherever I may be, and has enjoined upon me prayer and almsgiving throughout my life.

He has made me dutiful toward my mother, and He has not made me arrogant or wicked. Blessed was I on the day I was born, and blessed I shall be on the day I die and on the day I am raised to life again.'"

Hearing these words of the Quran, the King began to

cry. He cried so much that his beard was soaked in tears!

The King said, "What you have just recited must have come from the same source from which the words of our master Jesus Christ have come!"

Then, he turned to the Quraysh delegation and said to them, "You go back from here. I will never hand the Muslims over to you."

But the men who had been sent by the Quraysh did not accept defeat. The next day, they returned to the King's palace. They lied to the King that the Muslims had said very harsh things about Jesus Christ. They said that he should call them and ask them about this.

The King called the Muslims again and asked what they had said about Jesus. Jafar answered, "We said the same as our Prophet told us. According to him, Jesus was a servant and a Prophet of God. He was the Spirit and the Word of God."

When the King heard this, he said that Jesus was exactly what they had said about him!

Hearing the King say this, many of his courtiers were annoyed. But he did not pay any attention to them.

Then, the King told the Muslims that they could live in his country in peace and security. He would not let anyone harm them, even in exchange for a mountain of gold!

The King ordered all the gifts the Quraysh had given him to be returned to them. When the court was adjourned, the Muslims left the palace happy. On the other hand, the delegation of the Quraysh came out feeling humiliated.

This group of Muslims lived in peace in Ethiopia. When the Prophet migrated from Makkah to Madinah, most of them went back to Arabia and headed for Madinah. Afterwards, in the seventh year after the Prophet's migration, the remaining members of this group of Muslims, including Jafar ibn Ali Talib, also shifted to Madinah.

It is narrated in some books that the King of Ethiopia testified to the prophethood of the Prophet Muhammad ﷺ and that he uttered

the shahadah in the presence of the Muslims.
When the Muslims were preparing to return to
Madinah, he gave them money for their journey.
He told them that when they arrived, they
should request the Prophet Muhammad ﷺ to
pray for forgiveness for him.

When the Muslims arrived in Madinah and
told the Prophet about this, the Prophet rose
and performed ablution and prayed three times,
asking Allah to forgive the Ethiopian King.

When the Quraysh failed in their efforts
to bring back the Muslims who had gone to
Ethiopia, they started to vent their anger on the

handful of Muslims who were left in Makkah. Abu Jahl was the leader of the opponents of the Muslims. The Quraysh tried in every possible way to stop the Prophet's mission. But when they failed in doing so, they finally decided to boycott the family of the Prophet.

Accordingly, they prepared a Boycott Declaration, which they hung on the inner wall of the Kabah. It was like an official announcement to all the people of Makkah. According to this Declaration:

1. No inhabitant of Makkah was allowed to talk to any Muslim, male or female.

2. No inhabitant of Makkah was allowed to shake hands with any Muslim.

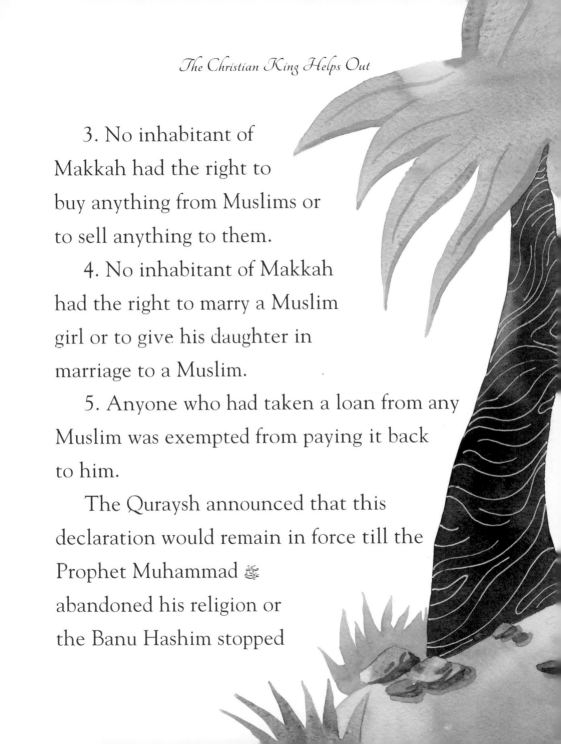

3. No inhabitant of Makkah had the right to buy anything from Muslims or to sell anything to them.

4. No inhabitant of Makkah had the right to marry a Muslim girl or to give his daughter in marriage to a Muslim.

5. Anyone who had taken a loan from any Muslim was exempted from paying it back to him.

The Quraysh announced that this declaration would remain in force till the Prophet Muhammad ﷺ abandoned his religion or the Banu Hashim stopped protecting him, so that the Quraysh could kill him. The text of the agreement was written up by a man called Mansur ibn Ikramah. The agreement was sealed with wax and hung inside the Kabah.

Abu Lahab, the leader of the Quraysh, was an uncle of the Prophet. At the same time, however, he was the Prophet's worst enemy. He led the whole tribe in planning new ways of troubling the Prophet and his family. Nobody was allowed to buy anything from them, to sell anything to them or even to visit them.

In those days, it was very difficult for a person

to survive without the support of the locally
dominant tribe. Without its protection, it was
difficult to survive. When the elders of the
dominant tribe turned against somebody, nobody
would talk to him. No one would offer him
water or food. No one would allow him into
his shop. And so, finally, he would have to bow
down to the tribal leaders. He would have listen
to them and do exactly as they wanted.

The Quraysh's hatred for the Prophet and
Islam was so strong that soon the Prophet,
his wife Khadija and their children, and Abu
Talib and his family and all the others who had
accepted Islam were forced to leave their homes
in Makkah. They took refuge in an open plot
of land called Shi'b Abi Talib, which was just

outside the town. There were no proper houses there, and so they had to live in tents.

It was like a refugee camp, and the family of the Prophet had to stay there for almost three years. They faced hunger, disease and poverty. Sometimes, they ate leaves from trees to satisfy their hunger, for there was hardly anything else to eat.

Khadija, who was not from the Banu Hashim, could have stayed on in Makkah. But she chose to stay with the Prophet in those difficult times. Once the richest lady of Makkah, she now lived in a makeshift tent under the open sky, without enough food and water. But she did not complain. She bore her difficulties with great patience. Her presence was a great support to the Prophet.

The inhabitants of the makeshift camp lived in great poverty. They wore old clothes and slept on old blankets. They had hardly any personal belongings. Khadija had just a wooden bucket and a mug. One day, the mug broke. She did not have enough money to buy a new mug for herself, and so she remained patient about it. Luckily, a carpenter was passing her tent and agreed to repair it for her.

The family of the Prophet survived the boycott only because once a year, during the four sacred months, they were allowed to go

to Makkah. These months were: Muharram, Rajab, Dhul Qadah and Dhul Hijjah. In those months, enmity with others and fighting were not permitted. Taking advantage of this, members of the Prophet's family would go to Makkah during these months and obtain food. They would get dried meat and the skins of animals that had been sacrificed at the Kabah and make them last for many days. They would boil the leather and chew on it to fight the pangs of hunger.

One night, Hakim ibn Hizam, Khadija's nephew, was taking some food for her. Abu Jahl, leader of the Quraysh, saw him going out of town and asked: "Where are you going?"

Hakim ibn Hizam truthfully answered: "I am going to meet Khadija to give her some food."

Abu Jahl got angry. He snatched the food and shouted: "You cannot take anything to the Banu Hashim! It is forbidden!"

Just at that moment, a man called Abul Bakhtari, who was not a believer, was passing by. He saw what had happened. He was a kind man, and he rebuked Abu Jahl: "Why do you stop him? What harm will be done if he takes some food for his aunt?"

This little incident led to a great argument and much discussion in the town. More and more people, horrified at the fate of the Banu Hashim, began to think and speak like Abul Bakhtari.

Finally, the boycott was lifted and the boycott notice was removed from the wall of the Kabah.

The family of the Prophet and some Muslims who were living in makeshift tents outside Makkah were allowed to return to their homes in the town.

But most of their houses were in bad shape— the roofs and walls were full of holes, wild weeds were growing in the cracks, and birds nested in the rooms.

The boycott that they had faced had not only been a physical punishment for the family of the Prophet. It had caused their economic ruin, too. Other Muslims, too, faced the same fate. Their businesses had been destroyed. Their entire savings had been quickly used up, and they were now on the verge of bankruptcy. It was very difficult for them to rebuild their lives.

At around this time, Abu Talib, the good uncle and great supporter of the Prophet for many years, became sick and weak. He died soon after the boycott ended and the Muslims returned to Makkah.

Khadija's health was not good either. She had suffered great hardship. Instead of herself eating, she used to give all the food to her children and husband. She passed away a few days after Abu Talib's death. Thus, two of the Prophet's most loyal supporters, who had stood like rocks behind him, suddenly left him. The Prophet was heartbroken.

He called that year "The
Year of Sorrow". Later
on, whenever he spoke of
Khadija, it was with great
love and fondness.

Khadija's life is a source
of great inspiration to the
believers, especially women.
She is an excellent example
of how one can give one's
time, energy, wealth and life
to the cause of Islam. Her
story is a reminder to the
believers to live a purposeful
life. We should remember
Khadija and the whole family

of the Prophet in our prayers for their sacrifices and dedication. It was precisely their sacrifices, dedication and hard work that enabled Islam to reach all the corners of the world and also enabled the Quran to be preserved in its original form.

Soon after the death of Abu Talib, the Quraysh redoubled their attacks against the Prophet. One day, one of them threw soil on his head. When the Prophet reached home, his daughter Fatima was moved to tears by the sight of her father. She washed and cleaned his head. The Prophet calmed Fatima by saying, "Don't cry, O Fatima! Your father has Allah for Protector."

After the death of Abu Talib, Abu Lahab became the chief of the Banu Hashim clan of the Quraysh. Since Abu Lahab was the bitterest enemy of the Prophet, his becoming the chief of the clan proved to be very hard on the Prophet.

Although Abu Lahab had agreed to lift the boycott under pressure from the people, his burning hatred for Islam still remained.
He convinced his fellow clansmen to expel the Prophet from their clan.

Once the Banu Hashim clan agreed to expel the Prophet, Abu Lahab, being the head of the the Banu Hashim, lost no time in announcing this to everyone.

In those days, a person who had been expelled from his tribe was regarded as someone whom anyone could kill. No one would take revenge for his murder. Anyone could enslave him.

After the Prophet had been expelled by the Banu Hashim, he found himself all alone. This happened when the two most important people in his life, Abu Talib and Khadija, had passed away. After their deaths, there was no one in Makkah to support and protect him.

When Abu Lahab expelled the Prophet from the Banu Hashim, all of a sudden the Prophet found himself alone, without any helper or supporter. Earlier, when the Prophet would reach home bleeding all over, Khadija, his loyal wife, would dress his wounds and comfort him with her kind and soothing words. In the same way, the Prophet's uncle, Abu Talib, would encourage him in his work. But when both of them passed away, the Prophet found himself helpless and all alone. Yet, he carried on with the dawah mission for which God had sent him.

During the Hajj season, the Prophet went to meet with the different tribes who came to Makkah. He went to their tents and requested them to take him under their protection so that he could continue his mission of conveying to people the message of the Quran.

One tribe that the Prophet approached was the Banu Amir. But they responded by throwing stones at him.

Another tribe that the Prophet approached was the Banu Maharib. But they refused to give him protection because they feared Abu Lahab.

During the Ukaz fair, which attracted people from various places, the Prophet met members of the Banu Kindah tribe. He said to them, "I call you to the One God, and I call you to protect me as you protect your lives." But they ignored the Prophet's call. They gave him no response. Then, the Prophet approached yet another tribe, but they responded to the Prophet's request with these words: "Neither will we turn you away, nor will we believe in you." This meant that they were not interested in his message, but that they would also not insult or humiliate him in the way that others had done.

In this way, no tribe agreed to provide shelter to the Prophet. No tribe was willing to take him under its protection, without which it was impossible for him to carry on living in Makkah.

At that time, it so happened that a group of people from the Banu Khifah tribe visited Makkah to perform Hajj. The Quraysh paid a sum of money to a man from this tribe to assassinate the Prophet. However, the Prophet got to know about this. And so, on the same night, he left Makkah for Taif, along with Zayd ibn Haritha, who was one of the first converts to Islam and the Prophet's adopted son.

اللَّهُمَّ أَطْعِمْ مَنْ أَطْعَمَنِي
وَاسْقِ مَنْ سَقَانِي.

O Allah, feed those who have
fed me and satiate those who
have satiated me.

"It is as bad as a lie if a person speaks about everything he hears without being certain of its veracity."

Muslim

Islam Begins to Spread in Madinah

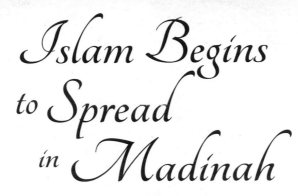

Taif is a city up in the mountains, about a hundred kilometres south-east of Makkah. The people of Taif were prosperous and wealthy. They had lush orchards, which produced a lot of fruits. They also engaged in money-lending, charging a very high rate of interest on loans. In those days Taif was also home to the only physician in the entire South Arabia. His name was Harith ibn Kaldah. The most renowned astrologer in Arabia also lived in Taif. His name was Amr ibn Amiya.

In Arabic, the word taif means "wall". There were walls all around Taif to make it safe from outside attack. That is how the town got its name: "The Walled City".Among the inhabitants of Taif at that time were three brothers, Abd Yalayl, Masud and Habib. They were well-known and respectable people. The Prophet thought that if they agreed with him, the entire town would agree with him, too.

And so, he travelled on foot all the way from Makkah to Taif, along with Zayd. It was a long and tiring journey, as the route passed through hilly and rocky countryside.

The Prophet and Zayd kept walking for days, crossing massive stretches of mountainous terrain. Finally, they reached Taif. They were exhausted, because it had been a long journey. The Prophet first went to see the three brothers. He was hopeful about them, as they

were relatives of Abdul Muttalib, the Prophet's grandfather. But, contrary to what he had hoped, they gave him a very disappointing reply. Abd Yalayl said, "Has God sent you as a prophet to disgrace the Kabah?"

One of his brothers added, "Could God not find anyone else to make His Prophet?"

And then the third brother said, "It is against our honour and dignity to talk to a person like you!"

Stunned by the response of the brothers, the Prophet left them with a heavy heart. He was very sad. He met some other people in Taif, but all of them gave similar insulting replies to his request for shelter and protection. No one received him as a guest. Instead of offering him food and water, they forced him to leave the town immediately.

When the Prophet was leaving Taif, the townspeople incited street urchins to throw stones at him and drive him out of the town. They hurled abuses at him.

Zayd tried to protect the Prophet by wrapping his mantle like a shield around him. But the Prophet was hurt so badly that his entire body, from head to toe, was bleeding. Blood trickled down from his body and started to fill his shoes.

Many years later, the Prophet narrated his journey to Taif to his wife Aisha and said, "The most difficult day of my life was that day in Taif."

In this way, the Prophet had to leave Taif with his entire body covered with deep wounds. He almost fainted. He sat down on the ground, unable to walk anymore. But the urchins did not let him sit and rest. The Prophet got up again and started walking, and the urchins continued throwing stones at him.

After a while, the sun started to set. It began to get dark. It was evening now, and the urchins of Taif slowly started to return to their homes.

The reason why the people of Taif mistreated the Prophet so badly was because they had come to know that he had been expelled from his clan, the Banu Hashim. And so, they got a free hand to humiliate him. They thought that they

could harm him in any way they liked. They knew no one would come to his aid.

Stumbling and limping, the Prophet moved slowly with the help of Zaid. He was in great pain, being hardly able to walk. So, he sat down on a rock by the wayside. In front was a vineyard that belonged to two brothers, Utbah and Shaybah. They were residents of Makkah. The Prophet went into the vineyard and took shelter in its cool and refreshing surroundings.

At that moment, moving words of prayer poured from the Prophet's lips, expressing his helplessness and suffering.

The Prophet raised his hands towards heaven and prayed: "O Allah, please take into account my feebleness, my poverty and the scant respect

that people have for me. O, Most Merciful God, Lord of the downtrodden, You are my Lord. My fate is in Your hands. My fate cannot be left to a stranger who hurls insults at me or to a foe who overcomes me. I long for You not to be angry with me. My sole aim is to please You. The light of Your faith banishes the darkness. This world and the next depend upon this divine light. I too seek refuge in its illumination and pray that You will not heap Your wrath upon me. Only You have the right to accuse and punish at will. No one has the same power and strength that You have."

The owners of the vineyard noticed that the Prophet was in great pain. They took pity on him. Out of compassion, they sent him a bunch of fresh grapes on a tray through their servant, Addas. This man was a Christian. The Prophet uttered the name of God before he began to eat the grapes. "In the name of Allah", he said.

"That is not what the people here usually say," Addas remarked.

The Prophet asked Addas about his religion and where he was from.

Addas answered, "I come from Nineveh, and I am a Christian."

"Are you, then, from the city of the Righteous Jonah, son of Matthew?" asked the Prophet.

Addas was surprised and asked in amazement. "What do you know about Jonah, son of Matthew?"

"He was my brother," said the Prophet.

"He was a true prophet, and so am I," the Prophet added.

In 800 B.C, the Prophet Yunus (Jonah) ﷺ who belonged to the Binyamin (Benjamin) tribe, was sent to the people of Nineveh, a very ancient town near the River Tigris, opposite the city of Mosul and approximately 230 miles north-west of Baghdad, in present-day Iraq. The ruins of the city can still be seen. The Prophet Yunus asked them to leave their old ways and follow the laws of Allah. But they did not listen to him and made a mockery of him. This angered the Prophet Yunus. He then left the city, discouraged by the failure of his mission, and boarded a ship. The ship was struck by a violent storm. He was thrown into the ocean by the others on the ship. Later, he was swallowed by a big fish and stayed inside it until he realised his mistake and sought God's forgiveness.

Overwhelmed with emotion, Addas began to kiss the Prophet's hands and feet. Right then, he accepted Islam at his hands.

The owners of the vineyard were surprised at seeing their servant kissing a stranger. When Addas returned to them, they came to know about his having accepted Islam.

The Prophet and Zayd rested in the vineyard for a while and cleaned and dressed their wounds. Later, they set out on the tiring journey on foot back to Makkah.

The harsh experience in Taif was the most difficult moment for the Prophet.

The Prophet's wife Aisha tells of how once she asked him, "O Messenger of Allah, has there been a more difficult time for you than Uhud?"

Uhud was the place near Makkah where a historic battle was fought between the Makkans and the Muslims. In this battle, the Prophet and many of his Companions suffered serious injuries.

The Prophet replied that the Makkans had inflicted many hardships on him. But the most

difficult day for him, he said, was the day when
he met Abdul Yalayl in Taif and had returned in
grief. The Prophet related to Aisha that when
he reached Qarn al Tha'alib, a place outside
Taif, he felt a little better. Then, he raised his
head towards the sky, for a cloud was giving him
shade. Then, the angel of God, Jibril, called
out to him, saying, "O Muhammad, Allah has
heard the reply which your people gave you.
Now Allah has sent the Angel of the Mountains

along with me. Whatever order you want to give him, please do so. He will obey your order."

Afterwards, the Angel of the Mountains, Malak al-Jibal, came before the Prophet. The angel greeted him and said, "O Muhammad, Allah has sent me to you. I am the Angel of the Mountains. All these mountains are under my control. Whatever order you like to give me, I will obey it. If you like, I can bring these two mountains together in such a way that the people of Taif get crushed between them."

The Prophet stretched his hands towards the sky and said, "No!" adding, "I am hopeful about their later generations. I am hopeful that the people who will be born in their next generations will not be like them.

They will worship Allah, and will not associate anyone with Him."

The Prophet's visit to Taif took place three years before his migration to Madinah. On the way back from Taif to Makkah, the Prophet stopped at a place called Nakhla.

The Prophet was worried about his return to Makkah. It was very likely that the Makkans would have come to know about the bad treatment he had received at the hands of people of Taif. For this reason, they might become even more aggressive in their opposition to him.

At Nakhla, the Prophet began to pray. As the Prophet was reciting the Quran in his prayer, a group of jinn passed by. When they heard the

Prophet's recital of the Quran, they stopped and listened to it attentively.

When these jinn returned to their people, they began to convey the message of the Quran to them. This incident took place without the Prophet's knowledge.

Later, a revelation of the Quran informed him about what had happened.

"It has been revealed to me that a band of the jinn listened [to the Quran] and they said, 'We have heard a really wonderful recital, which guides to the right path; so we have believed in it and we will not associate anyone with our Lord—and exalted is the majesty of our Lord— He has taken neither a wife nor a son.'" (Al-Jinn, 72:1-3)

After making this long, tiring and difficult journey on foot, the Prophet returned to Makkah. But he did not enter the town. He stopped at the Cave of Hira, outside the town.

At the instigation of Abu Lahab, the Banu Hashim had expelled the Prophet from the clan. In that tribal age, a person who had no protection from any tribe could not live in his village or town. Anyone could harm him or even kill him without fear of retaliation from his family or tribe. It was for this reason that the Prophet stopped at the Cave Hira. He sent word to two influential members of the Quraysh tribe, Akhnas ibn Shariq and Suhayl ibn

Amr, to provide him protection so that he could enter Makkah. But they did not agree to this. The Prophet then thought about Mutim ibn Adi, a man who had helped him earlier. Mut'im had played a major role in ending the boycott against the Prophet and his family.

The Prophet sent word to Mut'im about his return from Taif and requested him to provide him protection at that difficult moment.

Mut'im immediately agreed to this, and sent his six strong sons, fully armed, to escort the Prophet and bring him back to Makkah.

The first thing the Prophet did on entering Makkah was

to go around the Kabah seven times. This is known as *tawaf*. Mut'im announced, "I have given protection to Muhammad. Beware! No one should hurt him."

Because of the protection given by Mut'im, the Prophet once again had the opportunity to carry on with dawah work in Makkah.

Mut'im died before the campaign of Badr without accepting Islam. Hassan ibn Thabit, one of the Companions of the Prophet, wrote a *marthiya*, a poem in which dead people are remembered and praised, on the occasion of Mut'im's death. At the time of the Battle of Badr, when prisoners of war were brought before the Prophet, the Prophet said, "If Mut'im ibn Adi had been alive today and had asked me to release these prisoners, I would have done so."

During this period in Makkah, the Prophet married Sawda. Before her marriage to the Prophet, Sawda had migrated to Ethiopia along with her husband. But her husband accepted Christianity there. And so, Sawda got divorced from him and returned to Makkah.

Before the advent of Islam, fairs and festivals were organized in and around Makkah. The beginning of the month of Dhul Qada was when the famous fair of Ukaz was held. After this fair, people would go to the fair of Majannah, which lasted for three weeks. This was followed by the Dhul Majaz fair, which was organized during the Hajj season. The main attractions of these fairs were poetry recitation, storytelling and wrestling. People from far and wide would come to take part in these fairs and festivals.

The Prophet started visiting these fairs in order to preach God's message to the people who had gathered there. He would go to each tribe and convey to them the message of Islam.

One of the Companions of the Prophet

relates an incident that happened before he had entered the fold of Islam.

He says, "Once, when I was in the bazaar of the Dhul Majaz fair, I noticed a young man, covered in two red Yemeni sheets, passing by me. He was saying loudly, 'O people, say, 'there is no deity other than Allah' and you will be successful.' People were gathering around him to listen to what he was saying. Then, I saw another man, who was walking behind him. He was throwing stones at him, which seriously injured his legs and caused them to bleed. This man was saying, 'O people, this man is a liar. Do not listen to what he says!' I asked people, 'Who is this man?' They said, 'He is Muhammad. He belongs to the Banu Hashim. He claims to be a prophet.' The people also told me that the man who was walking behind him and throwing stones at him was Abu Lahab, his uncle."

In this way, the Prophet would go to fairs and convey the message of the Quran to the people gathered there, even if he had to encounter stiff opposition. In those days, Madinah was known as Yathrib. It is located about 400 kilometers to the north of Makkah.

There were many Jewish tribes living in and around Madinah at that time. In the sixth century B.C., king Nebuchadnezzar of Iraq attacked Palestine and destroyed Jerusalem. He exiled the Jews from there. Then, some of the Jewish tribes travelled to Arabia and settled down there, in places such as Khaybar and Yathrib.

It is said that about 120 years before the birth

of Jesus, there was a massive flood in Yemen, due to which the inhabitants of that area left and settled elsewhere. Among these people were two brothers, whose names were al-Aws and Khazraj. Along with their families, they settled in Yathrib. They worked there as farmers. Slowly, their offspring multiplied, and, after some generations, they formed two big tribes, known as al-Aws and Khazraj.

The Jews of Yathrib would hire people from these tribes as labourers to work in their fields. Apart from this, they would lend them money at a high rate of interest. Although the Jews were very powerful economically, they were not so strong in terms of manpower.

Whenever there was a conflict between the Jews and the al-Aws and Khazraj, the Jews would frighten them by telling them that a prophet would soon appear, and that, with his help, they would fight and destroy them!

In the eleventh year of the Prophet Muhammad's prophethood, some people from the al-Aws and Khazraj tribes received the Prophet's message during a trip to Makkah that they had made for performing Umrah, the 'minor pilgrimage'. When they saw and heard the Prophet, they were reminded of their Jewish neighbours, who used to tell them about a prophet who would appear in Arabia.

One of them said, "He seems to be the same prophet whom the Jews used to speak of."

Accordingly, six men from Yathrib accepted Islam right there and then. Their names are as follows:

1. Abu Umamah Asad ibn Zararah
2. Auf ibn Harith
3. Rafi ibn Malik
4. Qutbah ibn Amir
5. Uqbah ibn Amir
6. Jabir ibn Abdullah

In the following year, in 621 A.D., when people from Madinah came to Makkah for Umrah, the number of Muslims among the Madinans rose to twelve. They reached Makkah and met the Prophet at a place called al-Aqabah. They consulted him about dawah work in Madinah. This incident is known in the history of Islam as "The First Covenant of al-Aqabah." In entering into this covenant, they agreed on the following things:

1. That they would not worship anyone other than the one God.
2. That they would not steal.
3. That they would not commit adultery.
4. That they would not kill their children.
5. That they would not falsely accuse anyone.
6. That they would follow the Prophet's commandments in performing good deeds.

When these people were leaving for Yathrib,

the Prophet sent two men with them—Mus'ab ibn Umayr and Abdullah ibn Umm Maktum. These two men had learned the Quran by heart and could recite it in a beautiful voice. The Prophet thought they would help others in preaching Islam. They travelled to Yathrib and stayed at the house of Asad ibn Zararah, who had accepted Islam the previous year.

The situation in Yathrib turned out to be favourable for the preaching of Islam. Living along with Jews, the people of the town were acquainted with the notion of "the Prophet who was about to come." When they saw that the Prophet they were waiting for had been born among neither Jews nor Christians but among the Arabs, they were overjoyed. Up till then, they thought that they were inferior to the Jews, as the Jews had a Divine Book and they did not. But now they would believe in the Prophet Muhammad and would become possessors of the Divine Book.

اَلْحَمْدُ لِلَّهِ الَّذِي اَطْعَمَنَا وَسَقَانَا وَجَعَلَنَا مِنَ الْمُسْلِمِيْنَ.

All praises are due to Allah who provided us with food and drink and made us believers.

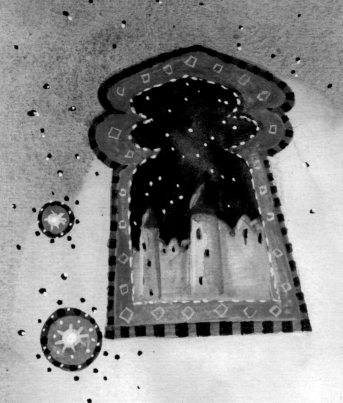

"Hell lies hidden behind evil
(worldly desires) and paradise is
screened behind hard labour."

Bukhari

The *Journey* to the *Seven Heavens*

The Prophet Muhammad ﷺ was given propethood in 610 AD in Makkah. After 13 years of peaceful dawah work, the Prophet had to migrate to Madinah, which is called Hijrah, or migration. About one and a half years before the migration, the Prophet had a very unique experience. The Quran calls it al-Isra and in the Hadith it is called Mi'raj.

The incident took place after the death of the Prophet's wife, Khadija. It took place on 27 Rajab in the tenth year of the prophethood, that is by the end of 620 AD.

The purpose of Isra, or Mi'raj, was that through such experiences Allah showed His prophets many of His signs which an ordinary human being cannot experience in this life, such as, how this universe is working, what is the

reality of the creation. And the reality of the Hereafter, Paradise and Hell. Allah has shown such extraordinary signs to His prophets.

The Quran says about the Prophet Ibrahim (Abraham) ﷺ, that "We showed Ibrahim Our kingdom of the heavens and the earth, so that he might have certainty of faith." (Al-An'am, 6:75).

In the same way the Prophet Musa (Moses) ﷺ was called by Allah up on to Mount Sinai and shown some of the most amazing signs of Allah. (Ta Ha, 20:2).

The purpose of showing these extraordinary signs to the prophets was that they could have complete faith in and commitment to their dawah work.

The incident of Mi'raj took place at night. The Prophet was sleeping in the house of Umm Hani, who was the daughter of Abu Talib and the sister of Ali ibn Abi Talib. Her house was very near the Kabah.

The Prophet was not in a deep sleep. It was a condition between sleep and awakening. He

 saw that the Angel Jibril (Gabriel) along with some angels had come. The Angel Jibril woke him up and took him

to the nearby well of Zamzam. He washed the Prophet with the water of Zamzam. Afterwards, a small animal, similar to a mule was brought, which was white in colour. It's name was al-Buraq. The Prophet rode this animal, and al-Buraq flew at lightning speed. It brought the Prophet from Makkah to Jerusalem in the twinkling of an eye, though the distance between Makkah and Jerusalem was about 2500 km.

The Prophet prayed two rak'ah (units) at the spot where Al-Masjid al-Aqsa stands today in Jerusalem.

Then the Prophet moved away from there and the Angel Jibril offered him two cups. One was full of milk and the other one had wine in it. The Prophet accepted the cup with the milk. To which Jibril said, "You preferred to be true to your nature. If you had taken the cup filled with wine, you would have gone against your own nature."

Afterward the Angel Jibril took the Prophet Muhammad ﷺ along with him and flew towards the sky. When Jibril reached on the First Sky, he called out to the angel who was there

on duty. "Who is it?" asked the angel. Jibril told him his name. The angel said, "Who is with you?" Jibril replied, "The Prophet Muhammad,

upon whom be
peace." The angel asked, "Has
he been invited?" Jibril said, "Yes." Then
the angel opened the door and said happily,
"Welcome, the people of the sky will be pleased
to hear this news."

The Prophet now entered the First Sky. He
saw a man, who had various shadows on his left
as well as on his right. When that man looked to
his right, he would laugh and when he looked to
his left he would cry.

When he saw the Prophet Muhammad ﷺ, he said, "Welcome O righteous Prophet, O righteous son."

The Prophet asked Jibril, "Who was that man?" "He was your father, Adam," replied Jibril. Jibril explained that the shadows on his left and on his right were that of his children, the entire humanity. On his right, the shadows belonged to those whose souls would enter Paradise. While on the left, the shadows belonged to those who would go to the Hell.

When he looked to his right, he laughed and became happy. While when he looked towards his left, he cried and became sad.

Afterwards, the Prophet saw two rivers. The Prophet saw another river as he walked further ahead. Jibril told the Prophet, "This is the river Kawthar, its soil is like musk."

In the same way the Prophet passed through all the skies and met with several prophets. The Prophet Muhammad ﷺ met with the Prophets Isa (Jesus) عليه السلام and Yahya (John) عليه السلام in the Second Sky.

In the Third Sky, the Prophet Muhammad ﷺ met with the Prophet Yusuf (Joseph) عليه السلام. In the Fourth Sky the Prophet met with the Prophet Idris عليه السلام. In the Fifth Sky, the Prophet met with the Prophet Harun (Aaron) عليه السلام.

All the Prophets greeted him by saying, "Welcome, O righteous Prophet, O righteous brother."

In the Sixth Sky, the Prophet Muhammad ﷺ met with the Prophet Musa (Moses) ﷺ.

In the Seventh Sky, the Prophet met with the Prophet Ibrahim (Abraham) ﷻ, who greeted

him by saying, "Welcome, O righteous Prophet, O righteous son."

The Prophet Ibrahim ﷻ was sitting at al-Bayt al-Ma'mur, which was a house in Paradise like the Kabah. 70,000 angels entered it every day. (The Quran uses this name, al-Bayt al-Ma'mur, for the Kabah in Makkah, meaning, the inhabited house, which is frequented by people all the time.)

Then, the Prophet Muhammad ﷺ was shown the Paradise. Its dome was made of pearls and its soil was that of musk.

The Prophet walked further and reached as far as *al-Sidrat al-Muntaha* or the Furthermost Tree. This was a Lote tree, which was the last destination beyond which no creature can pass. The tree was emitting beautiful and colourful lights all around it. This was the place from where Allah's decisions descend. This was also the place from where the deeds, accounts, prayers, etc, of the people go up.

After reaching this point, the Angel Jibril took on his original form.

At this moment the Prophet Muhammad ﷺ saw the splendid light, which was the Light of Allah.

At this moment, Allah revealed some important commandments to the Prophet Muhammad ﷺ.

The Quran describes the incident as follows:

"He was taught by (an angel) who is mighty in power, and endowed with wisdom; who in time manifested himself; standing poised at the highest point on the horizon, then came down close until he was two bow-lengths away or even closer and revealed to Allah's servant what he revealed. The heart (of the Prophet) did not misconstrue what he saw. Will you then dispute with him as to what he saw? And certainly he

saw him descend a second time: by the lote-
tree of the farthest limit, beyond which none
may pass into the Garden of (Eternity) Repose,

when the lote tree was covered in mystic splendour. His sight did not waver, nor was it unduly bold. He saw some of the greatest signs of his Lord." (Al-Najm, 53:5-18)

According to the Hadith, these revelations were about the following three things:

1. The five daily prayers or Salat.
2. The last portion of the surah 2: al-Baqarah.
3. Verses 27-39 of surah 70: al-Isra'.

These revelations were similar to what the Prophet Musa (Moses) ﷺ received on Mount Sinai, known as the Ten Commandments.

Afterwards the Prophet returned to the earth. He then entered Jerusalem. Here he saw that all the prophets were gathered. He saw that the Prophets Ibrahim عَلَيْهِ السَّلَام and Musa عَلَيْهِ السَّلَام were praying. The Prophet described the physical appearance of some of the prophets that he saw there. For example, about the Prophet Musa عَلَيْهِ السَّلَام, he said that he was tall, he had curly hair, and his complexion was wheatish.

About the Prophet Isa (Jesus) عَلَيْهِ السَّلَام, he said that his height was medium, his complexion was fair, his hair was straight and long. He was looking very fresh, as if he had taken a bath a short while ago.

The Prophet said that the physique of the Prophet Ibrahim ﷺ was quite similar to his own.

It was time to pray the dawn prayer or fajr. The Prophet Muhammad ﷺ lead all the prophets in prayer. This was a symbolic act meaning that the chain of prophets that had been started with the Prophet Adam ﷺ had now ended with the Prophet Muhammad ﷺ. No more prophets would now come after the Prophet Muhammad ﷺ.

The mission of the Prophet Muhammad ﷺ was the same as that of all the prophets. This was to bring the divine message to all people: this is called dawah work.

Afterwards, the Prophet woke up and found himself near the precincts of the Kabah, exactly at the spot where he had been sleeping.

This experience cannot be explained in human terms, as this was a miracle. We can only partially understand it, as man cannot understand these hidden realities which are beyond space and time.

The Prophet told of his extraordinary experience to the people in Makkah, but most of the people there refused to believe him. Only the Sahabah or the Companions of the Prophet believed in what the Prophet said. It became a source of conviction to them and strengthened their *iman*, or faith.

The leaders of Makkah said to the Prophet, "O Muhammad, you say that you went to Jerusalem in one night and returned the same night." "If this is true," they continued, "then tell us what Jerusalem looked like."

The Prophet became a little nervous, as he did not remember how the city of Jerusalem had looked. In his anguish, the Prophet Muhammad ﷺ prayed to Allah for help. All of a sudden the Angel Jibril appeared to him, but only the Prophet was able to see him.

The Angel Jibril brought in his hands the map of Jerusalem, which he put in front of the Prophet (the map was visible only to the Prophet).

The leaders of Makkah kept on asking the Prophet about Jerusalem and he replied to them by looking at the map brought by Jibril.

Allah's purpose of Mir'aj was to show the Prophet a glimpse of the Unseen World. As the Quran says: "We might show him some of Our signs." (Al-Isra, 17:1)

Among these signs, there were things such as angels, Paradise and Hell, etc. Allah shows His prophets these signs through direct observation, so that their conviction and realization may increase and they may do their mission of dawah work with full devotion and dedication.

However, there is another very important sign in the Night Journey. Allah showed through this unusual

303

experience that an age will come when speedy travelling by aeroplane and fast communications will become a reality. All these things which we now know of in as the age of communication, were hidden from the world.

Through this unique experience, the Prophet was indirectly told that though the situation in Makkah seemed very difficult and hard to bear, and though the people of Makkah failed to understand the message of the Prophet, a time would come when the mission of the Prophet would reach far and wide and would enter each hearth and home on the globe.

Therefore, the Prophet said that there would not be a single home or hearth left

on the face of the globe where the word of Islam would not enter. This was a prediction made by the Prophet, that in future, fast ways of communication such as the internet and travelling by aeroplane would enable believers to engage in global dawah work. The religion of Islam, which was started in Makkah, would reach every nook and corner of the globe with the help of global communications. Due to this, not a single human being – male or female – would remain unaware of the message of the Quran.

The experience of the Night Journey and Ascension (Isra and Mi'raj) is, on one hand, a prediction and good news for global dawah work and, at the same time, it points towards

an immense opportunity which has already become a reality. Now it is the duty of all the followers of the Prophet Muhammad ﷺ to use all forms of modern communications and deliver the message which the Prophet Muhammad ﷺ brought in the seventh century to everyone on the globe.

The Prophet Muhammad ﷺ realized that it was impossible to do dawah work in Makkah. So in the thirteenth year of his prophethood, he decided to shift to Madinah. This event is known in Arabic, as Hijrah, which means, the Migration.

Just before the Migration, the Quraysh tribe, which was opposing the Prophet, held a meeting at al-Dar al-Nadwah, or the Tribal Parliament.

All the important leaders attended it. They said that despite their efforts to stop the Prophet, his mission was spreading in and around Makkah. The leaders all expressed their views on the subject, and wanted to find ways to stop his mission.

One of them said, "Let's put Muhammad in chains and imprison him." Another said, "No need to do that, we should expel him from Makkah." Many others suggested how they should stop the Prophet from spreading his mission in and around Makkah. But none of these suggestions were agreed to. Finally, Abu Jahal suggested that the Prophet

be assassinated. He said, "Let's select one youth from each tribe and tell them to attack Muhammad collectively."

"In this way, no one will be held responsible for the murder," he added.

The leaders of the Quraysh agreed to this cruel suggestion. The Prophet's aunt came to know about the evil plan of the Quraysh and she rushed to the Prophet's house to inform him about it. The Prophet immediately started planning to migrate from Makkah to Madinah.

Three days before the migration to Madinah, the Prophet left his house in the afternoon to meet Abu Bakr. After reaching his house, the Prophet knocked on the door, and when he got the permission to enter, he went inside the house. At that time Abu Bakr was sitting on a cot. He got up and asked the Prophet to sit where he was sitting.

The Prophet said, "I need to discuss a very important issue with you, so ask everyone to leave." Abu Bakr said, "There is no one except my two daughters in the house," meaning, Aisha and Asma.

The Prophet told Abu Bakr that Allah had given him permission to migrate to Madinah.

Abu Bakr said, "May I accompany you on this journey?"

"Yes," replied the Prophet.

Since Abu Bakr already had an

inkling about the migration, he had arranged to keep two white and very fleet-footed she-camels some days prior to the Prophet's visit.

Abu Bakr fondly fed them babool, or gum Arabic tree leaves. He offered one of these she-camels one of to the Prophet. But the Prophet said, "I will accept it only if you sell it to me. I will pay the price."

Abu Bakr reluctantly sold one of the she-camels to the Prophet. Her name was Qaswa.

Then Abu Bakr told his elder daughter, Asma, to prepare some food for the journey.

Asma prepared some food and dates, etc., and put everything in a sack. Then she wanted to tie up the open end of the sack. She searched for a rope, but could not find one. She had a rope tied around her robe. So she removed it and tore it in two. With one half she tied up the sack containing the food for the Prophet. The other half she tied around her waste again. For this reason, Asma is remembered as "the one of two ropes", or zat al-nitaqain.

Even before the Prophet told him about the migration from Makkah to Madinah, Abu Bakr had been in contact with a person known as 'Abdullah ibn Urayqit.

'Abdullah ibn Urayqit was a guide and an expert on desert routes. So Abu Bakr hired him as a guide to assist them on the route from Makkah to Madinah, as they planned to travel by a route which was different from the usual one. The Prophet left Abu Bakr's house and reached his home. He called 'Ali ibn Abi Talib and told him that he would leave for Madinah that very day. The Prophet had a sheet from Yemen, which had green lines on it. He gave it to 'Ali and told him to sleep on his bed at night and cover himself with this Yemeni sheet.

The people of Makkah were against the mission of the Prophet but, at the same time, they trusted him and called him Al-Amin, the Honest One. So, they would give him their valuables, such as jewellery, etc. for safe keeping.

Then the Prophet told 'Ali to return all the valuables which had been left with him for safe keeping to their rightful owners.

The Prophet then left for Abu Bakr's house. At night the Prophet and Abu Bakr quietly left the house through the back door.

Both of them quietly set off on foot for the Cave of Thawr, about 3 kilometers south of Makkah. This cave is on top of the Thawr Mountain, which is about 1000 meters high. One can see the Red Sea from its summit.

As they were leaving the house, Abu Bakr called Abdullah ibn Urayqit and handed over the two camels to him. He told him to bring the camels to the cave of Thawr, in three days' time. As per their plan, the youth of the

Quraysh tribe encircled the house of the Prophet with swords in their hands. They all decided to wait till the morning as they were expecting the Prophet to come out of his house for the morning prayers. They thought that when the Prophet came out, they would all attack him with swords. It was against the Arab culture at that time to attack someone inside his house. So they waited till the break of the dawn. But, the Prophet did not come out of his house. They peeped inside the house and saw someone was sleeping on the bed. They thought the Prophet was sleeping. They waited. But, after a while, Ali ibn Abi Talib got up and came out of the house.

At that time, they came to know that the Prophet was not in his house. They detained

Ali in the Sacred Mosque for a while, then they let him go. Afterwards, they went to the house of Abu Bakr, and knocked on the door. Abu Bakr's daughter, Asma came out. They asked, "Where is Abu Bakr?" "By God, I don't where are they now," replied Asma. Abu Jahl, who was also there among the people, got angry when he heard this. He slapped Asma and went of hurling abuse at her.

Before leaving his house, Abu Bakr told his

son, 'Abdullah to keep a secret watch over what was happening in Makkah and then inform them about this at night in the

Cave. Abdullah did as he was told. He watched the people of Makkah quietly and every night visited the Cave of Thawr to inform his father about any new development which had taken place in Makkah. Abu Bakr also told his servant, Amir ibn Fuhayrah, to come close to the Cave with his goats so that they could have their milk.

When the people of the Quraysh came to know that both the Prophet and Abu Bakr had already left Makkah, they became very furious and red faced. So they immediately sent out several search parties to catch the Prophet and Abu Bakr, before they could reach Madinah.

They searched for the Prophet everywhere. Some of them even came close to the cave in which the Prophet and Abu Bakr were hiding. Abu Bakr heard the crunching and rustling noises of grass and weeds as the people approached the cave. He became very frightened and said to the Prophet, "It seems that they have even come this yarn." Seeing Abu Bakr so frightened, the Prophet replied calmly, "What do you think about the two, with whom the third is Allah?"

"Don't be sad, Allah is with us," said the Prophet, comforting him.

Though the search party almost right up to the entrance of the Cave, did not go inside and went off disappointed. The Quran records this incident in Al-Tawbah, 9:40.

The Prophet Muhammad ﷺ and Abu Bakr remained in the Cave for three nights. On the fourth day, the Prophet and Abu Bakr came out of the Cave. Abdullah ibn Urayqit was already there with the two white she-camels.

Then the Prophet set out on his journey to Madinah. Abdullah ibn Urayqit, mounted on his camel, led the small caravan. The Prophet rode on the next camel. On the  third camel, Abu Bakr and his servant, Amir bin Fuhayrah were mounted. So this was a caravan of three camels and four people.

They continued travelling for the whole day. Abdullah ibn Urayqit was an expert on desert routes. He took the Prophet by an unknown route, not the one which was commonly in use.

He took the Prophet along the banks of Red Sea. Through this was a longer route, it was safe, as no one would follow the Prophet along this unknown path.

After a long journey they finally reached Madinah safely.

اللَّهُمَّ اغْفِرْلِي وَارْحَمْنِي
وَعَافِنِي وَاهْدِنِي وَارْزُقْنِي.

O Allah! Forgive me, have mercy on me, heal me, guide me, and provide sustenance for me.